ROADSIDE FLORIDA

Solomon's Castle, Lily.

ROADSIDE FLORIDA

The Definitive Guide to the Kingdom of Kitsch

Peter Genovese

STACKPOLE
BOOKS

Published by
STACKPOLE BOOKS
5067 Ritter Road
Mechanicsburg, PA 17055
www.stackpolebooks.com

Printed in China

10 9 8 7 6 5 4 3 2 1

FIRST EDITION

Design by Beth Oberholtzer
Cover design by Caroline Stover

Library of Congress Cataloging-in-Publication Data

Genovese, Peter, 1952–
    Roadside Florida : the definitive guide to the kingdom of kitsch / Peter Genovese.
    — 1st ed.
        p.   cm.
    Includes bibliographical references and index.
    ISBN-13: 978-0-8117-0183-9 (pbk.)
    ISBN-10: 0-8117-0183-2 (pbk.)
    1. Florida—Guidebooks.   2. Florida—History, Local—Guidebooks.   3. Road-side architecture—Florida—Guidebooks.   4. Historic sites—Florida—Guidebooks.
5. Curiosities and wonders—Florida—Guidebooks.   I. Title.

F309.3.G46   2006
917.5904'64—dc22
                                                        2006010579

Contents

Flamingo Inn, Grassy Key.

Goofy Golf, Panama City Beach.

Introduction

This book is the result of thousands of miles driven through Florida over the period of a year and a half. I did little research before setting out. This may sound like heresy, or sheer stupidity, but bear with me a moment.

I did consult the indispensable roadsideamerica.com website for obvious must-sees like the world's largest gator, in Kissimmee, and the nation's smallest police station, in Carabelle. Mostly, though, I drove around the state and discovered things on my own. I wanted to be surprised. I wanted to see things fresh, through my eyes and not someone else's.

SunSationS, Panama City Beach.

I was looking for colorful roadside art and architecture, but even that description comes up short. Other books, such as *Florida Curiosities*, by David Grimes and Tom Becnel, and *Oddball Florida*, by Jerome Pohlen, have nicely covered the strange and eccentric side of Florida—unusual museums, famous graves, and other roadside oddities.

Roadside Florida covers some of this ground, but I was more interested in everyday roadside whimsy: funny signs, unusual store facades, roadside murals and sculpture, colorfully named towns, vintage motel and restaurant signs, roadside giants, one-of-a-kind buildings, and so on.

When I set out on the road, I didn't really know what I was looking for, but I knew it when I saw it. Kitsch, eye candy, roadside color—call it what you want, Florida fairly explodes with the stuff. I doubt any other state has a more vivid and thriving roadside culture; nearly every bend in the road promises a new treat.

Some places were obvious chapters. How can you ignore the World's Biggest Orange or the one and only Solomon's Castle? Some places were not. A bar may not seem like a proper subject for a book like this,

"Gifts" boat, north of Crystal River.

Paradise Inn, Kissimmee.

but once I visited Jimbo's in Virginia Key, I knew it was a perfect fit. Gatorama is not really an example of roadside art or architecture, but no book about the Florida roadside would be complete without a nod to the state's colorful roadside attractions.

Several leads came from published accounts. I first read about Dave Shealy and his search for the skunk ape in a *Miami Herald* story. I knew I had to include Ruby Williams after reading a piece about her in the copy of *Forum* magazine shown to me by Donald Ferguson, the subject of another chapter.

You might ask, "What's a guy from New Jersey doing writing about Florida?" I've written extensively about Americana. My first book, *Road-*

side New Jersey, explored my native state's roadside culture. I spent a year and a half driving up and down U.S. Route 1 for *The Great American Road Trip: US 1, Maine to Florida*. I spent a year visiting every diner in the Garden State for *Jersey Diners*. I also write regularly for *American Road* magazine.

Put me on a highway, show me a sign, and I'm a happy guy.

After all my Florida travels—four separate road trips in 2005 alone—I feel confident in saying I've seen more of this state than most Floridians. I've been to nooks and crannies many Floridians have never even heard of, much less visited. You name the town, chances are I've been there. Plus, I've vacationed in Florida since college spring break days. Don't ask me about that period of my life; I plead the Fifth.

You won't find any haunted houses or headless nuns in these pages, no midgets, mummies, or madmen. There are no Elvis or UFO sightings, no uninhabited graves or assorted bumps in the night. If you want fiction, look elsewhere. Inside these pages are real people, real stories, real life. *Real* Florida, or at least the non–Chamber of Commerce Florida. Enjoy!

The World's Biggest Orange

"I'm here to see Eli," I tell the attractive blond-haired woman behind the counter at Orange World.

"Did you bring a ladder?" Kathy Franco asks.

"Uh, no," I reply, puzzled.

I've gone to some lengths, and heights, for interviews, but this is the first time anyone has asked me to bring a ladder to one. I tell Kathy I'm here to interview her father, Eli Sfassie, the man behind the World's Biggest Orange. Eli shows up half an hour later, says hi to his daughter, spots me, and says, "Did you bring a ladder?"

They have mistaken me for a contractor who is scheduled to take a look at bumps and bruises in the giant orange's fiberglass sheath. The contractor shows up ten minutes later, and yes, he's brought his ladder. He and Sfassie promptly head up the ladder to the roof.

Eli Sfassie, proprietor of Orange World.

Orange World, 5395 West Irlo Bronson Memorial Highway (Route 192), Kissimmee.

"When people ask where I work, I tell them the big orange," says Karen Potocnak, who works in the gift shop.

You might need to shield your eyes the first time you walk into the shop, and not because of the lighting. She and Franco wear orange sweatshirts so blindingly bright they are probably visible out to sea. "The joke around here is, Where are the batteries?" Karen says, laughing.

Born and raised in Kissimmee, Karen is a natural for Orange World. Working in a roadside attraction that consists of a humongous piece of fruit requires a sense of humor, if not an incredible amount of patience.

"This guy walks in one day with his wife," Karen says. "He asks, 'Where's that big orange?' I said, 'You're standing in it.' He turns to his wife and said, 'See, I told you there was no petrified orange that big.'"

Karen and Kathy can reel off trivia about oranges faster than you can peel one. The World's Biggest Orange is ninety-two feet wide, sixty feet high, and weighs thirty-five thousand pounds. It's painted every three years; the job requires fifty-five gallons of paint. The most common question asked is, What's upstairs? Answer: Air, mostly. Operating hours are 8 A.M. to 11 P.M. seven days a week. Orange World is closed just one day, Christmas. Hundreds of thousands of oranges are shipped from here every year. The people at Orange World don't grow the oranges; they come from different groves. The packing house, run by Orange Ring, is on Highway 27 in neighboring Polk County.

"There are 104 kinds of oranges," Kathy says. Navels are her favorite. "They're seedless, and they've got bigger pulp. They're the best."

She and Karen sing the juicy praises of tangerines, Valencias, and especially honeybell tangelos, which many regard as the sweetest, juiciest citrus fruit of all. They're available in January only.

Word of warning to first-time visitors to Orange World: This isn't Fruit World. "We do not carry bananas; we carry only citrus," Kathy points out.

Kathy Franco and Karen Potocnak.

East Sugarland Highway, Clewiston.

Lake Placid.

If you want a nice picture of the colossal citrus, bring a professional camera; that little digital doohickey of yours might not do it justice.

"It's funny watching people trying to take pictures of it," Kathy says. "You can't get the whole thing in unless you stand in front of it. So we give them a free postcard."

Orange World is located on Highway 192, probably the most kitsch-crazed of all Florida roads. When Orange World was built, none of the castles, giant alligators, wand-wielding wizards, and other wonders now along the road were in existence. "Back then, it was just orange groves and cattle," Karen recalls.

"It was nothing, just trees," says Sfassie, back in his office after his rooftop expedition. "I grabbed ahold of Disney's shirt and didn't let go."

He bought the business from a previous owner; a contractor "kind of convinced" him to build the dome. "He said he could put it up, no problem," Eli recalls. "The only thing he was building with fiberglass was outhouses." He smiles. "I don't think so."

The project didn't go smoothly and delays caused locals to derisively call it "Eli's Folly."

"That big crane," Eli says, pointing to an old snapshot, "cost $875 a day, sitting on the ground. The minute the crane touched the material the wind came up. It was almost like the Good Lord didn't want me to put the sucker up."

Disappointed—"I knew it wouldn't be finished in time for Christmas"—Eli walked into the Waffle House next door. Sitting at a booth were six ironworkers.

"I asked them, boys, are you looking for work? I told them what I needed done. They called their boss. He said, 'yeah, go ahead, make some Christmas money.' They said, 'We'll do it, as long as you throw in a couple cases of beer.' They jumped on that damn thing, put it up in two days. No price was spoken; whatever they were going to charge, they were going to charge. The next day, I went back to the Waffle House, asked them, what do I owe you guys? They said, give us $1,000 each. I went to the bank, withdrew $6,000 in $100 bills."

State Road 17, Sebring.

Goulds.

It was the best $6,000 he ever spent. The giant orange increased business fivefold.

"It's a landmark; even airline pilots can see it," he says. "It's a gimmick world. You gotta go with the flow. If you don't, the world will pass you by. If this was just a gift shop, we wouldn't succeed. A billboard on this highway costs $3,000 a month. That's $35,000 a year."

"For many people, it's the first stop when they visit the area," Karen says. "It's the only place around you can get fresh-squeezed orange juice."

But fresh-squeezed juice must be kept below 45 degrees, or the container, after an hour or so, will begin to swell. Then it can explode. Karen can speak from personal experience; a container of fresh-squeezed once blew up, covering her from head to toe in orange juice.

The store is a souvenir hunter's vision of paradise, with a staggering array—even by Florida gift shop standards—of T-shirts, sweatshirts, shorts, caps, snow globes, preserves, pencils, orange gum, orange blossom perfume, canned Florida sunshine, and other gotta-have items. If you buy $100 worth of fruit, you get a free World's Largest Orange T-shirt.

In the movie *Marvin's Room*, starring Meryl Streep, Leonardo DiCaprio, Diane Keaton, and Robert DeNiro, there is a scene where several characters drive in front of the World's Biggest Orange. They "make a turn and they're in Daytona Beach," says Karen, shaking her head.

Eli says the fiberglass orange is largely maintenance-free, except for the occasional bump and bruise. Kathy and Karen think the dent in the fiberglass that the guy with the ladder is here to fix was caused by the ball once held by the wizard atop the gift shop down the road. The wizard stayed put, but his ball has not yet been found.

Eli, his time with the ladder guy finished, hops in his car and drives off. An employee carefully arranges the pyramids of glistening oranges outside. Inside, Kathy and Karen get back to the business of running the World's Biggest Orange. The days are long, and you have to worry about such occupational hazards as exploding OJ, but these girls know how to have fun.

"I'm buying Kathy a redneck spa treatment for Christmas," Karen whispers to a friend over the phone. "A six-pack of Corona and a bottle of Calgon."

Men from Mars

First of all, let's set the record straight: The men from Mars, who work in a body shop of the same name in Dade City, really are from Mars.

Mars, Pennsylvania, that is—about thirty miles north of Pittsburgh. Northeast of Moon, southeast of Energy, west of Apollo, if you must know.

"We sat around one day trying to think of a name. It was Mars, we're from Mars, then it was Men from Mars," says James Irvine.

Call him ringleader of the Men from Mars. Irvine was the first one of the crew to move down there. "It was divorce, get out of town, one of those deals," he says laconically. Over the years, he persuaded his buddies from back home to join him.

"I used to twist a wrench. I used to work for his dad," says Ed Foster, maybe the most loquacious of the Men from Mars. Among other jobs over the years, Foster painted water towers. He

Men from Mars Automotive, Highway 301, Dade City.

Ed Foster (above); James Irvine (right).

Ace and Rich Fiel.

started coming to Florida in 1991. He's not from Mars but Zelienople, Pennsylvania, about halfway between Mars and Big Beaver. I'm not making any of this up; other towns in the vicinity include Economy, Industry, Dime, Distant, and Oklahoma.

It took Irvine a while to find his calling in the Sunshine State. The first winter, he sold Christmas trees. Or tried to. He loaded up a school bus with one thousand trees and sold about half, barely making his money back. "I made the mistake of coming down too late," he said. "If we had been here two weeks earlier, we'd have been fine."

He eventually opened up the shop on Highway 301. The Men from Mars do custom painting and body repair, specializing in classic cars. "We do a lot of work on older cars," Irvine explains. "We just did a '69 Firebird. We have a '67 Firebird convertible. We just did a '69 Chevelle. There's an old Cutlass."

Irvine, a pleasingly pudgy guy partial to flannel shirts, owns a 1969 GTO. He and his fellow Martians—Foster, Rich Fiel, and a guy named

For your car in Miami.

Ace—do much of the work outside, in the shade of a towering oak. "That's the hood off our spaceship when it landed," cracks Fiel, pointing to a pickup hood painted in bright green flames.

"Service out of this world; prices down to earth," announces Irvine's business card.

On the battered garage door is a plaque that reads "Mars Pennsylvania 1873, 1973 Centennial." There's a painting of a pointy-eared alien with "Hi, I'm Jim" underneath it. A yellow sign warns: "Dog on Guard 3 Days a Week. Guess Which Days."

Irvine might have wanted to sic the dog on the guy who showed up one cold (for Florida) December day. The power—and heat—had been knocked out. The Men from Mars couldn't whistle while they worked; they were too busy shivering. It was a $600 job; the customer picked up his car but never paid.

"Last time I do something like that," Irvine mutters.

But work is steady under the big oak tree, and it sounds like the Men from Mars have finally found a home.

"We wanted something catchy, something people would remember," Irvine says. "People say, those guys from outer space, the guys from Mars, fixed my car."

Bithlo.

Solomon's Castle

The castle shimmers in the late afternoon sun. Which it should, considering it's made of shiny newspaper printing plates. Two knights stand guard at the castle's entrance. Igor the iguana, whose favorite food is mac and cheese, lolls in a circular cage that wraps around an oak tree. Inside the castle are mermaids, unicorns, elephants, giraffes, and lions, all made from scrap—master cylinders, oil cans, toilet valves, pump handles, and whatever else the castle's owner can scrounge up. Like the eighty-six cans of Schmidt's beer he used to make a chair.

Nearby is a sixty-foot replica of a sixteenth-century Spanish galleon. On the other side of a moat—patrolled by a gator—is an open-air dining room perched above an expanse of swamp and forest. A lighthouse pokes its way skyward.

The castle, boat, and lighthouse were all made by one man, equal parts folk artist, eccentric genius, and comedian. "This is my source of inspiration," the castle's seventy-year-old owner says, pulling up the top of an American-flag-decorated figurine in his living room to reveal a bottle of Smirnoff's.

He leads the way past a wall covered with nothing but woodworking planes into his travertine-floored kitchen. He points out the massive dumbwaiter and cracks, "I used to take people up there until their husbands complained."

How about the Blue Room, where guests can spend the night and tell friends back home they stayed in a castle? "It's $125 a night," he says. "For an extra $50, I put on a French maid's outfit and do room service."

It's a joke, but with this guy, you never know.

"My name is Howard Solomon," he says at the beginning of a tour. "Welcome to my castle."

Of all the offbeat attractions in Florida, there is none more unlikely than Solomon's Castle. It is located in Lily, which is down the road from Ono (the castle's mailing address), which is pretty much near nothing. It's just an hour east of Bradenton, but once you approach Lily, you need to make several turns down backroads; keep your eyes peeled for the small homemade signs.

Finally, though, the castle appears in a clearing, a shiny fortress with towers and parapets—but no fair maidens, unless you count Solomon's offer to dress in the French maid costume.

"That balcony," he says, standing on the front lawn, "is where I stand and speak to all my subjects on any subject."

Solomon's family was from Siberia. He grew up in Rochester, New York. After high school, he ended up in Largo, Florida, where he learned boatbuilding and cabinetmaking. Then it was on to Freeport, in the Bahamas, where he opened an artist's workshop.

"Tiring of coping with the changing political tides," Billie Solomon Cohen writes in *The Story of Solomon*, a children's book, "he returned to Florida, looking for a quiet sanctuary in which to continue his art, away from the madding crowd."

He found it in Lily. Solomon bought forty acres in 1972, when land was $350 an acre. In 2004, he bought the adjacent orange grove for $10,000 an acre. The property is now ninety acres in all. When he and his first wife first moved here, they lived in a mobile home on the grounds. Now he and his second wife live in the castle, which they are only too happy to show you.

The castle also doubles as museum and art gallery for Solomon's fantasy pieces, all made from junk and scrap. There is a grouper made from oil cans; a tractor made of master cylinders; a Fulton Fish Market truck

Solomon horse.

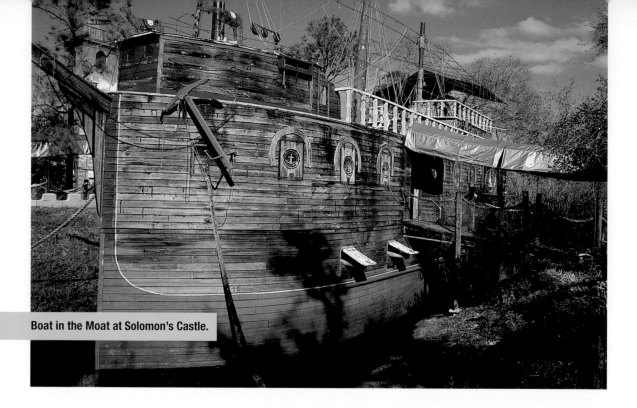

Boat in the Moat at Solomon's Castle.

fashioned from newspaper plates; a menagerie—unicorn, elephant, giraffe, penguin—made from coat hangers; guns fashioned from pieces of hacksaw, toilet valves, pump handles, and pipe wrenches; and that eighty-six-beer-can chair. Lionel the Lion is built out of five oil drums and seventy pounds of welding rod; a six-foot-high elephant on wheels, fashioned from seven oil drums, took Solomon three hundred hours to build.

"Brake shoe period. 1973–74," proclaims a sign.

The lord of the castle is a short, gnomish-looking man in a blue T-shirt, worn jeans, and owlish glasses. He's spry, sometimes profane, and often political. A machine gun on a wheeled cart, for example, is "a Kent State debating machine."

Bad puns are part of his schtick; his audience moans good-naturedly. "Oh, it gets worse," he announces. He points to a giant mousetrap: "a weapon of mouse destruction." And so on.

"This is where I live," he says, leading us into his cozy, carpeted living room. "I'm never late for work." There's a woodstove, vintage cameras on the shelf ("that's a picture window"), and views of woods. A formidable roll piano stands in a corner; the selection of boxes includes "I'll See You in My Dreams" and "Show Me the Way to Go Home." He pulls up a swatch of carpet and opens the door to his "dungeon," a basement where several mummified-looking dolls in distress, including a Red Hat Lady, peer out.

Diamond Castle, South Atlantic Avenue, Cocoa Beach.

Round Table Sports Bar and Lounge, Miami.

Beverage Castle, Highway 301 South, Harney.

DoubleTree Castle Hotel, International Drive, Kissimmee.

M. D. Custom Cycles, Overseas Highway, Key Largo.

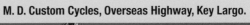

The ship, which took Solomon four years to build, may be even more remarkable than the castle. He built the ship's cannon out of irrigation pipe. The miniscaffold under the portholes, he says, was "for my wife, so she could wash the windows. That was the day she left."

Inside is a restaurant, the Boat in the Moat; the local UPS driver is in there today, enjoying a slice of pie. The restaurant has a full kitchen, stained-glass-window portholes, and seating for sixty; it is often rented out for private parties. The menu includes corned beef on rye, a barbecued pork sandwich, old-style meatloaf, chili, various salads, and "the world's best hot dog." Beers are $2.50. Desserts include Ace of Spades Chocolate Cherry Cake, Diamond Jacks Walnut Pie, and the Queen of Hearts Lily Lime Pie, made from limes grown on the castle grounds.

Later, Solomon invites me to jump into one of his five golf carts for a tour of the property. His daughter and son-in-law are building a bed-and-breakfast, the Horse Creek Life House, behind the castle. Each room boasts a Jacuzzi.

Nearby is his studio, a warehouselike space. He has sold his pieces all over the world, he says. He takes on one major commission a year, although he says he's constantly making smaller pieces.

A shed is jammed with junk: fifty pounds of military belt buckles; barrels overflowing with brake shoes and U-joints; shelves of railroad spikes; a vast assemblage of nuts, bolts, pipes, wire, bike rims, lights, switches, toilet valves, license plates; even an Erector Set from his childhood.

"People bring me junk," he says. "I wish they'd stop."

But stopping is one thing he doesn't plan on doing. "I'm afraid to," he explains. "I've seen people stop and they can't go on anymore."

He's not in perfect health; he's had two heart operations and now has emphyscma.

Last year, he attended his fiftieth high school reunion in Rochester. He says he had to crash it. "I didn't graduate," he admits.

Don't tell the lord of the castle he's in the middle of nowhere. "We're within an hour and a half of 80 percent of Florida's major cities," he cracks.

That's one way to look at it.

Many stories and programs have been done on the castle over the years. Of them, Solomon seems most enamored of a British TV special titled *Dumb America*, about various U.S. oddities. The castle, he says proudly, was the only thing they didn't call dumb.

The Nation's Smallest Post Office

How small is the nation's smallest post office? Just ask Nanette Watson, the postmaster. "The dimensions are exactly eight feet, four inches by seven feet, three inches. The peak of the roof is ten feet, six inches."

She sits behind the counter of the Ochopee Post Office on U.S. Highway 41, the Tamiami Trail, in the Everglades. If you didn't know any better, you'd think it was a shed, or maybe an ice cream stand, certainly not a thriving post office. It's located on a stretch of road that may see more gators than cars on an average day. The Tamiami Trail, so named because it runs from Tampa to Miami, was completed in 1928. A 49.5-mile segment southeast of Naples is designated a natural scenic highway. Scenic, if you like a whole lot of nothing. Scenic, if you like palmetto, sawgrass, and swamp stretching as far as you can see.

It's my kind of highway, and if you're reading this book, it's probably yours, too. In all, U.S. 41 runs 1,990 miles from Michigan to Florida. A sign at its northern terminus, in Fort Wilkins State Park near Copper Harbor, Michigan, traces its beginnings: "Early Indian footpaths became the trails for explorers, missionaries and fur traders who came to carve out homes in Michigan's wilderness. The early settlers began to widen and improve these trails, which became the majority of Michigan's primary road system."

Today that wilderness still can be found at the highway's southern end, in the Everglades. Royal Palm Hammock, Carnestown, Monroe

Station are little more than dots on the map and road. U.S. 41, which runs through eight states, ends in Miami. The Tamiami Trail, as the website seeamerica.org points out, "ends as it begins, with the culture and flavor of Cuba. What starts near Tampa's Ybor City, a vibrant cigar-rolling center in the early 1900s, stops just beyond Miami's Eighth Street—Calle Ocho, and the heart of Little Havana."

Ochopee, about seventy miles from Miami, might as well be on another planet. It's tiny, but not inconsequential. There's the post office, Dave Shealy's skunk ape headquarters, and landscape photographer Clyde Butcher's Big Cypress Photography studio, which includes these helpful directions from Miami: "The gallery is on the south (left) side of Tamiami Trail. There is a sign out in front. If the gallery comes up suddenly, do NOT slam on your brakes. You can drive one half mile further to the Big Cypress National Preserve Visitor Center and make a safe turn around at that location."

Google "shopping in Ochopee" and you'll get one listing: Joan's Kwik Stop Country Store. If you don't count things wrapped in plastic at Joan's, there's one restaurant: Joanie's Blue Crab Café, a short stroll from the post office. Joanie's—more shack than café—is the quintessential roadside dining and drinking experience, where gator tail, soft-shell crabs, and Seminole fry bread are menu staples and you help yourself to beer from a cooler. Chelle Koster Walton, in a *Miami Herald* story, included Joanie's among a dozen classic Florida "get-down, down-home" restaurants "that have survived the onslaught of chains and fancy-schmancy to serve up a taste of local color along with their y'all-come brand of cuisine."

Skunk ape headquarters, Joan's Kwik Stop, and Joanie's—that's Ochopee. The community center, such as it is, is the post office, open from 10 A.M. to noon and 1 to 4:30 P.M. Monday through Friday and 10 to 11 A.M. Saturday.

Tiny post office, big route: The lone carrier, according to Watson, drives 135 miles every day, six days a week, making 350 stops. Watson has worked in Ochopee eleven years; previously she was in the Boca Grande and Everglades City post offices.

"Ochopee was a very big place in the fifties and sixties," she says. "There were three general stores, a cement operation. There were tomato fields." Asked for more details, she laughs. "I wasn't born yet; you've got to give me a break!"

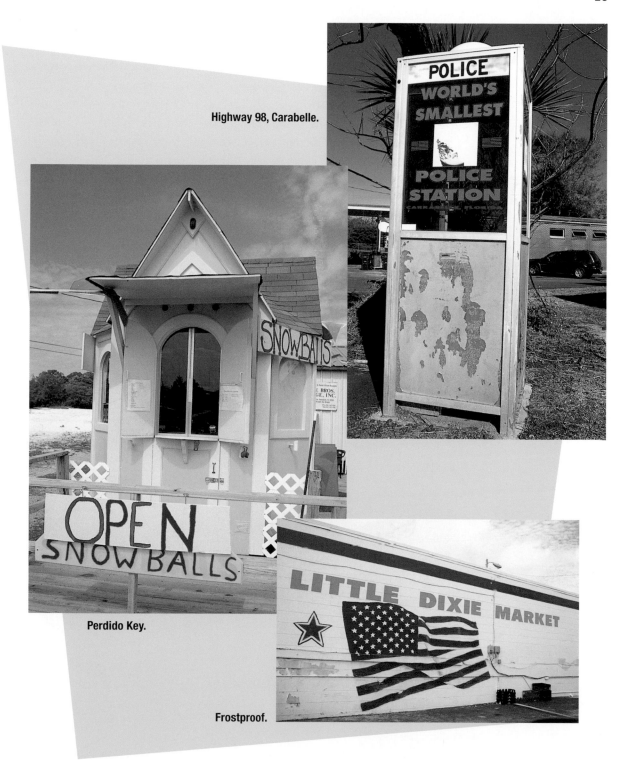

Highway 98, Carabelle.

Perdido Key.

Frostproof.

The building, according to the marker out front, was once an irrigation pipe shed owned by the J. T. Gaunt Co. tomato farm. It was "hurriedly pressed into service" by then-postmaster Sidney Brown after a disastrous fire burned down Ochopee's general store and post office in 1953. The present post office has been in service ever since, serving customers, including Seminole and Miccosukee Indians, in three counties.

Two locals, Sidney Brown and a Mr. Cail, built shelves and cubbyholes to hold the mail, according to florida-everglades.com. When the Tamiami Trail was widened, the building was moved back on a wheelbarrow to its current spot.

The cubbyholes are still there, and Watson is on hand to answer any and all questions. "Bus tours always stop here," she says. "It's their smoke break."

Among her visitors this day are Alex de Quesada of Miami and his seven-year-old daughter, Nikki. Wearing a T-shirt that reads, "Buy Me Something," she takes a minute to write an important postcard.

"Hi, Mommy," it begins. "I'm in the smallest post office in the United States. I'm having a lot of fun and I went to the Everglades. I saw 19 gators. Daddy saw 22."

Cocoa Beach.

Between the Buns

He's played trumpet on Prince, Diana Ross, and Marvin Gaye albums and on several movie soundtracks. So what's John Leotine doing selling hot dogs in a parking lot in Orlando?

"I wanted to do something that was fun and simple and related to pop culture, Americana," he explains. "And I wanted to stand out."

That he does, working out of a ten-and-a-half-foot-high, twenty-five-foot long fiberglass hot dog stand. It's called Between the Buns, and it's located along Highway 50 in Orlando. Don't worry; you won't miss it.

"I wanted to go back to the time when your building was a sign," Leotine, fifty-four, says. "I realized this would bring people in and the quality of the food would keep bringing them back."

He sells quarter-pound hot dogs, plus burgers, fries, and soda, from Florida's biggest hot dog. He once thought about calling it Hot Diggity Dog, but he liked Between the Buns and the play on words.

"It's all about sex, drugs, and rock and roll," he says, laughing.

Once, it was all about music for him. A Boston native, Leotine started playing the trumpet when he was in sixth grade. After college, he moved to Los Angeles and found studio work with the likes of Prince and Diana Ross. He also contributed to several soundtracks, including "Children of a Lesser God" and "I'm Gonna Git You, Sucka."

But after a dozen years in La-La Land, it was time for a change. "I felt I was playing a dinosaur instrument. And things were slowing down a little bit."

Between the Buns, 646 West Washington Street (Highway 50), Orlando.

He moved back to Boston, worked for his brother's painting outfit, then as a cook in several restaurants. But freedom—and hot dogs—beckoned.

"Truthfully, I never ate many hot dogs before," he says with a laugh. "It was just that I wanted to do something simple. And I wanted to put a smile on people's faces. You see families breaking up all the time. I want to go back to a simpler, happier time."

He designed the giant hot dog, had "a fiberglass guy" in Boston build it, and trucked the mighty frank down to Florida. For the first four years, Between the Buns was located along International Drive in Orlando. For a year, it was stationed in front of a Harley-Davidson dealership.

Then Leotine decided he wanted to "get off the tourist track and get back into the community." He found his current spot, the parking lot of a gas station and convenience store on Highway 50.

"A lot of people come here because of me, my personality," he says. No kidding.

He looks like Billy Joel, talks like he's in a race against time, and can run rings around the Energizer Bunny.

"A lot of people say, 'I want to do what you do.' They think you can just throw something like this up." They don't want to hear about the 11- to 12-hour days and everything else that goes into running a one-man business. "Success comes on the back of hard work," he explains. "That's what separates the men from the boys."

Between the Buns is open every day but Sunday. Leotine sells 120 to 150 dogs a day. "That's all right," says the hot dog man, clearly wishing he could do better. "Remember, I'm by myself."

You can have your dogs three ways—grilled, broiled, or deep-fried— with various combinations of toppings. The Mexico City dog has ketchup, mustard, onions, mayo, bacon, and jalapeños. The Latin Lover comes with mustard, ketchup, red onion sauce, chili, and sauerkraut. The Texas

Highway 27, Clermont

Westville.

PORK
- PIG HEAD
- SALTED PIG TAIL
- SMOKED SHANK
- HOG JAW
- PIG EARS

Tampa.

Westville.

Miami.

Bull Dog combines barbecue sauce, melted cheese, bacon, onion, and jalapeños. The Rockin Rio, a Brazilian-style dog, throws together mayo, ketchup, corn, Parmesan cheese, and potato sticks. The Junkyard has a little bit of everything. Leotine is proudest, though, of his chili. "There are a thousand ways to make chili. I've got people who drive an hour to get my chili."

He uses quarter-pound Best's Kosher hot dogs from Chicago. "It's not for any ethnic reason. They're consistently flavorful. They're expensive, but my customers enjoy them. People say, 'Use any hot dog, they won't know the difference.' Bullshit. People know. You have to dazzle people with food, whether it's caviar or hot dogs."

One online reviewer, at orlandocitybeat.metromix.com, made note of the outdoor seating arrangements: "a couple of plastic chairs dangerously close to a major highway. But hey, what fun is life without the possibility of being creamed by oncoming traffic while stuffing your face with a quarter-pound hotdog?"

The seats are not that close to Highway 50. The bigger worry here is spending your entire lunch hour in line. It can get busy, and Leotine is a one-man operation.

"I've got New Yorkers—they smell the place, they say it smells like home," he says. "It brings people back to their childhood memories."

Next step? He wants to go nationwide, then worldwide, offering Between the Buns franchises. "I want to put one of these in Tokyo, I want to put one of these in London, I want to put one of these in Paris," the hot dog man says.

In the meantime, there's Orlando, and getting Between the Buns on the map.

"I have an ego; I need to be famous," Leotine says, laughing. "Damn it, I'm in showbiz! This is like L.A., only better."

Goofy Golf

Some wag once called miniature golf "the feeblest outdoor activity this side of waiting for a bus." The wag was wrong. Is any summertime activity more primally pleasing than putt-putt? Anyone can play, everyone has fun, and there is no danger of having sand kicked in your face, being eaten by a shark, or getting swept out to sea, all of which can happen on your typical day at the beach.

Today about ten thousand miniature golf courses can be found around the country. In 1930, there were up to *five times* as many. Blame it all on James Barber of Pinehurst, North Carolina. In 1916, Barber hired Edward Wiswell to lay out on the grounds of his estate a minicourse incorporating all the elements of "real" golf. In 1926, Drake Delanoy and John Ledbetter built New York City's first outdoor miniature golf course on the roof of a skyscraper in the financial district. The duo went on to open 150 rooftop golf courses in the city.

Minigolf became all the rage. It "breathed new life into a moribund economy," according to *Miniature Golf*, the wonderful book by John Margolies, Nina Garfinkel, and Maria Reidelbach. "The craze provided much-needed stimulus to such diverse industries as cotton, lumber, concrete, steel, roofing and lighting, and saved 100,000 workers from soup kitchens and bread lines." By 1930, an estimated four million Americans were out on any given night playing putt-putt. Department stores offered miniature golf outfits for men and women. Tournaments attracted top players from around the country. Someone even wrote a song, "I've Gone Goofy over Miniature Golf."

Sphinx at Goofy Golf, 12206 West Highway 98A, Panama City Beach.

There's no better place to go goofy than at Goofy Golf in Panama City Beach, across the street from the city pier and the Gulf of Mexico. Founder Lee Koplin picked the spot, figuring the pier's presence meant no one would be allowed to build a hotel and block the view.

In this age of thoroughly unadventurous Adventure Golf courses and less-than-lush Jungle Golf links, Goofy Golf stands as a testament to putt-putt's golden days. The course itself is rather ordinary—flat, straight, and uneventful. But the obstacles, and the time-warp feel, make Goofy Golf special. To some, Goofy Golf, which opened in 1959, may seem woefully old-fashioned. The figures look as if they have been pulled from a time capsule: an inscrutable Sphinx, a monolithic Easter Island head, an angry brontosaurus, a grinning red-eyed monkey, and a serene-looking golden Buddha, among others.

Today Lee Koplin's kids, Randy and Michelle, own Goofy Golf. They grew up in a house right on the property and had to walk around the

Purple dinosaur, Goofy Golf.

Buddha and an Easter Island head are among the exotic icons at Goofy Golf.

dinosaur's legs to reach the front door. Lee would take his son around the lit-up course at night, and Randy would say good night to the fish, the monkey, the dinosaur, and the rest of the minigolf menagerie.

Lee's dad was a welder who had gone west as a young man to work on the Hoover Dam. Goofy Golf's history is told in the excellent book *Florida's Miracle Strip: From Redneck Riviera to Emerald Coast*, by Tim Hollis. In 1948, the owner of a minigolf course in Guerneville, California, asked Koplin to build some statues for him. "According to family lore, the addition of the eye-catching statuary more than doubled the course's income overnight, and Koplin realized he might be on to something big—but he didn't realize how big," Hollis writes.

Koplin spent the next ten years traveling around the country, building miniature golf course obstacles. In the late 1950s, he opened a course in Biloxi and called it Goofy Golf. Koplin, according to Hollis, "was at one time troubled by nightmares in which he would be pursued by a wild assortment of terrifying monsters; he supposedly conquered this problem by turning the creatures into the most enjoyable part of his game."

Two other Goofy Golf courses were built, in Fort Walton Beach and Pensacola, but Koplin was not directly involved in designing them. The former was distinguished by a fearsome headhunter, who grasped a woman's disembodied head in his hand. Other figures included a tyrannosaurus, blue sailfish, elephant, kangaroo, and giraffe. The Pensacola Goofy Golf was built, according to a local newspaper account, by "a pair of carnival veterans, a redhead and a bald man."

In 1958, Koplin picked out his spot along a then-undeveloped stretch of beachfront in Panama City Beach. In his first few years of operation, Koplin added bigger and bigger obstacles, including the brontosaurus and the massive Easter Island head. A winding stairway in the latter leads to a small observation deck with panoramic views of the course and beach.

Postcards of the time show a wooden windmill fronted by a giant plastic tulip, a beady-eyed octopus clutching a willowy mermaid, giant butterflies, a red-sailed pirate ship, a castle with a moving drawbridge and flag-topped turrets, and other wondrous sights. The parking lot was sand; it is now paved.

An ad proclaimed: "It's Invading the Country. Official Goofy Golf. Panama City Beach, Florida. Fun and Skill for Everyone."

Behind the course, where Raccoon River Campground is today, was Tombstone Territory, a Wild West attraction. Wanna-be cowboys and cowgirls could ride a miniature train around the grounds, watch jailbreaks and gunfights, and eat all the ice cream their little stomachs could endure. There was a jail, general store, hotel, saloon, trading post, chapel, and Koplin's pièce de résistance, the monumental Cliff Palace, a replica of Mesa Verde in Colorado. Other entertainment consisted of cancan girls; one postcard shows the leggy performers in extravagant pinkish red skirts and enormous feather-topped hats.

Is it any wonder that Koplin's kids "felt something like Alice in Wonderland," as Hollis puts it. Goofy Golf spawned imitators: Sir Goony Golf, Zoo-Land Golf, even other Goofy Golfs that had no connection to the Koplins. Lee Koplin passed away in 1988, but Goofy Golf lives on.

"Though plenty of low-concept mini golfs and water parks now crowd Panama City Beach, Goofy Golf is content to be the one that never

Wild creatures at Goofy Golf.

changes," according to roadsideamerica.com. "The Johnny-Putt-latelys a few miles up the strip can't even tell you where Goofy Golf is located."

Harris Miniature Golf Courses in Wildwood, New Jersey, is the nation's largest builder of minigolf courses. The company has built courses around the world, from South Dakota to South Korea. The minigolf course at South of the Border is a Harris creation. One of Harris's more recent designs is the Hawaiian Rumble in Orlando. Flames appear to shoot out of a forty-foot-high volcano; a waterfall leads to raging rivers and spray fountains.

At the other end of the putt-putt spectrum is Goofy Golf, delightfully old-fashioned, wonderfully out of touch. It doesn't "belong" on the modern-day Miracle Strip, with its high-rise condos and high-tech water parks. But it has managed to survive, if not thrive, all these years. Next time you're in Panama City, stop by and play a round. Sneak up to the top of the tiki head if you can. And don't forget to say good night to the animals.

Ruby's Folk Art Is Very Very Hot

Don't blink, or you'll miss Bealsville. The town—a few modest homes, the Bealsville Church of God, the Glover School—is strung along Highway 60, fifteen miles east of I-75. Even Miss Ruby, who helped put Bealsville on the map, can be easily missed if you're racing past at fifty or sixty miles per hour.

There's no giant billboard advertising the wonders within Miss Ruby's roadside stand, no gaudy banners or brilliant neon. What you see, instead, are handpainted signs wedged amid the tomatoes, beans, peas, and sweet potatoes.

"Rubys Stop Now," says one.

"Ruby Say Thanks," reads another.

A black-lettered board in front of a tangle of onions makes this request: "Calling for All Saints to Please Pray Now."

Another sign, dangling from a fence, lets you know that the sweet, mild-mannered Miss Ruby is no pushover: "Please Shut Your Mouth."

"I do crazy signs," admits Ruby Williams, seventy-eight years young. "Once I made a sign that said, 'Ruby's 1,000 feets ahead,' "My family said, 'Why you do something crazy like that?' I said, 'Got your attention, didn't it?'"

She has gotten a lot of people's attention since she started selling her folk art along with the beans and peas years ago. The art is simple and direct, and it's often religious or inspirational in tone. Many works consist of words wrapped around someone's face or body. "Hey I Found Something" is the message on one, which directs you to a passage in the

Hey I Found Something.

Bible. "When We Forgive, We Free Ourselves from the Bitter Ties That Bind Us to the One Who Hurt Us" reads another.

"As a child, I couldn't dance, I couldn't talk," says Ruby, wearing jeans, white socks, dark brown boots, and a paint-splattered green-and-white-striped shirt. "They used to pick on me so much. But I knew I was different."

She was the third of seven children; her great-grandmother was one of five freed slaves who helped found Bealsville.

"When I was nine, I got saved, I got to know the Lord," she says. A brother and sister died when she was young. "I thought if they died, God kept me for something, I got something to do. Then you go seeking for what it is you have to do."

Born in Bealsville, she worked on a farm when she was a child. She picked berries, which is why, she says, there are so many berries in her paintings today. She married, divorced, and moved to New Jersey to join her sister, but she quickly skips through this part of her life as if it's not important. She worked at a funeral home, in an upholstery shop, and as a counselor to kids. She moved back to Florida in the mid-1980s and started to work the family farm once again.

"I took to raking and leveling off the land and put me up a produce stand," she recalls. She glances at the tin-roofed shack that doubles as produce stand and art studio. "The Lord is good to me, but I had no way of getting up there to make the roof." A neighbor did that.

She grows beans, greens, peas, onions, sweet potatoes, and strawberries "with water and loving kindness." She's up at 5 A.M., and when she's not working the field or talking to visitors out near the highway, she cares for a daughter, who recently suffered a stroke.

"You've got something inside you; you've got to get up and use it," she says, sitting on a plank. "You have to plant the seed in order to get something. I made up my mind: I'm going to be a winner."

Self-taught, she started painting in the late 1960s. Her first work consisted of a crude fish. She branched out to include others of God's crea-

Calling for All Saints.

tures, and she got better at it. A more recent painting shows a piano-playing cow happily announcing, "I Give Better Buttermilk." Another shows a red-beaked blue bird and the words "If I Can Do It so Can You."

The art world took notice, and Ruby's work started appearing at galleries both local and nationwide. The highlight came in 2004, when Ruby came to the Smithsonian's attention. She was part of a yearlong exhibit titled "On Their Own: Selected Works by Self-Taught Artists," sponsored by the Anacostia Museum and Center for African-American History and Culture, part of the Smithsonian. Her paintings now sell for hundreds or even thousands of dollars; they can be found in galleries and on the Internet, or you can just stop by Ruby's produce stand in Bealsville and buy one directly from the artist.

Her studio is a chicken coop–like enclosure jammed with works of art in all shapes and sizes and by turns playful, inspirational, solemn, and joyous. Most of the time she paints outdoors, using a paint-splattered wooden board as a table. Art is everywhere: in front of the vegetables, on a fence, stacked against a wall, on the ground.

"I like the sound of the highway for company," she told Kate Santich, writing for *Florida* magazine. "That's what I always said I wanted to do when I retired—to live beside the highway and be a friend to man."

She was no friend to the art dealers who bought her work for cheap and sold it for exaggerated prices. Williams, according to Santich, painted a work titled *Tired of Being the Good Guy*, "a speckled gator with long claws and sharp teeth and its tongue sticking out. She included the title on the canvas so no one could miss it."

Mercy and Truth.

You can buy a twelve-by-eighteen-inch version of that work for $375 on such Internet sites as visionaryart.com. Or you can just stop at Ruby's annual folk art bash, held the first Saturday of November. There is food aplenty and speakers. Admission is the grand sum of $1. Ruby gives the money to the men who help her on the farm.

It's doubtful art dealers are taking advantage of Ruby these days. Her work appears at House of Blues locations around the country, and she is one of the artists featured in the book *Just above the Water: Florida Folk Art* by Kristin G. Congdon and Tina Bucuvalas.

She's also the subject of a children's book, *I Am Ruby*, by Sylvia McCardel Thomasson, illustrated with Ruby's paintings.

"Can I buy it somewhere?" I ask her.

"Sure you can," she says. "Buy it from me."

Ruby is honest and direct—in her manner and her art. A sign propped against her goat fence reads:

No Drugs Here
Selling or Smoking Drugs Here
No Loud Noise
No Cursing or Being Nasty.

A giant ripe strawberry glistens on another board. "Rubys Folk Art Is Very Very Hot," trumpets still another. There's even a painting on her car's rear windowsill: "Today the Sun Don't Always Shine on You." Her initials, RCW, appear on all her works.

"Some of her savvy sayings are religious," according to southern visionaryart.com, "but most are moral lessons or are based on memories drawn from her life, some with a little 'attitude' thrown in for good measure."

A force of nature, she's been known to drive to St. Petersburg and drop off produce at local nursing homes. She goes to the bank and market just the way she is dressed now—jeans, boots, work shirt.

"The clothes don't make you," she says.

Ruby's Stop Now.

She washes her car—sometimes. "I don't care what it looks like, as long as it cranks up and goes."

She says she's "a businessperson, not a phone person," but she carries a cell phone in her dungarees. She pulls a pork chop from a bag and eats it for lunch. "I picked some okra this morning," she says. "I love it! Gonna get some potatoes, boil them down, have them for dinner. Oh, man!"

Strawberry season is coming, so she's fixing up her strawberry signs. "They don't like the heat. They're a cool kind of berry."

She says she enjoys "digging in the soil, cutting, and raking. It's all about getting my fingernails in the dust, get 'em down in the dirt."

She gets up; it's time to get back to work—the farm, not her paintings. Her secret to being active and alive? "You've got to eat sturdy food and be moving around and praying to God," Ruby replies. "Some people say, take things day by day. That's okay. But I say step by step, especially since I'm getting older."

This Place Bites

Allen Register strides down a winding, narrow, tin-roofed boardwalk, past fenced-in enclosures that are home to two sleek and silent Florida panthers, several African tortoises, bobcats, and coatimundis, plus a spider monkey named Willy and a capuchin known as Gizmo.

Register, in shorts and sturdy hiking boots, pauses in front of a low-walled pool that is vacant apart from some floating leaves. "Salty, here!" he shouts suddenly. There is nothing in the water; who is he talking to? A moment later, a reptilian shape, dark and sinister, glides slowly under an opening in the wall from the other side.

Say hello to Salty, a fourteen-foot saltwater crocodile. He's one of the main attractions at Gatorama, on Highway 27 in Palmdale. Register and his wife, Patty, own the classic roadside attraction, ringed by palms and oaks. Gatorama features the largest collection of large alligators

Feeding time at Gatorama, 6180 Highway 27, Palmdale.

and crocodiles in the world, plus the country's only breeding colony of alligators. "This Place Bites," announces a sign above the gift shop door.

Unlike Gatorland in Kissimmee, a short ride from Disney World, Gatorama is not on the way to anywhere. Situated just west of Lake Okeechobee, Gatorama is a step-back-in-time kind of place. The foliage, plus the screeching macaws and monkeys, make you feel as if you just came upon a tropical jungle.

"Take a short drive to the edge of civilization!" heralds a Gatorama brochure. "It still has the aura of the fifties and sixties," Allen Register says.

Patty's parents, David and Marietta Thielen, bought Gatorama from the original owner, Cecil Clemons, in 1986. "When he started it, it was

Allen Register with croc, Gatorama.

strictly for tourism," Allen explains. "He knew when Yankees came to Florida, they wanted to see alligators."

He and his wife expanded Gatorama's focus, increasing the harvesting side of the business. They harvest about one thousand gators a year, selling more than fifteen thousand pounds of meat annually. Most of the hides end up in Italy, France, and Japan. Crocodiles are a protected species, so croc is not on the Gatorama gift shop menu, and no croc hides are sold in the store. Allen holds one of thirty state gator farm licenses; the couple is the only producer of Florida gator meat.

You can pick up frozen gator from the Gatorama gift shop or order it on the Internet at gatorama.com. "The Finest Tail Anywhere," reads the label on two-pound packages in the gift shop freezer. They don't sell gator meat to restaurants, with one exception: the Double Muskee in Girdwood, Alaska.

"It's a high-quality product," Patty says. "We don't put fillers, chemicals, or additives in it." What does it taste like? "It's a very mild-flavored, sweet meat," she says. "It's not strange-tasting."

A *Miami Herald* story once described gator meat as "like a cross between mahi-mahi and catfish with a sweet hint of clam."

A sleepy crocodile at Gatorama.

Call it delicious. The gator bites that Allen fries up and brings back to the gift shop counter are terrific—and addictive. Patty's favorite gator recipe? Sautéed gator in garlic. "Cilantro and garlic and wine just simmering in there," she says, rolling her eyes. "You pour it over pasta. I love it."

You can pick up recipes for honey-grilled gator ribs and Granny's alligator chili at the gift shop. In addition to running the gift shop, Patty participates in the Florida Cracker Cooking School, a daylong trip run by Royal Palm Tours that makes five stops, including Gatorama.

"We've developed a reputation for being a foo-foo alligator farm," Patty says. Even she is not sure what it means, but it sure sounds funny.

Goliath, Gatorama's star attraction.

She is a local girl, Allen a Winter Haven native who served in the Navy. "Never in a million years did I think I'd be doing this," he says wryly.

About 3,000 gators and 200 to 250 crocs lurk about the property. Most of the gators are baby ones used for harvesting. The gators in the pens and lake will not end up as food or handbags; they're strictly for show purposes. There are about two million wild gators in Florida. There have been 342 documented attacks on humans by gators since 1948, with 20 fatalities, three in May of this year alone.

Along the pathway are several Cuban crocodiles, maybe the fiercest of all crocs; mugger crocodiles, with the broadest snouts; and panthers, of which there are maybe fifty to seventy-five in the entire state. There's Rambo, a thirteen-foot nuisance gator, and Mighty Mike, another thirteen-footer that had taken up residence in Lake Talquin, just west of Talla-hassee, where he had created a pest of himself. He was finally captured by Tony Hunter, one of thirty state-licensed nuisance gator trappers.

Hunter said he really hated to kill this croc. "Every year it gets harder for me to [have to] kill him. I hope somebody can keep him alive."

The star attraction, though, is Goliath, a fourteen-foot, forty-year-old crocodile that has been at Gatorama since 1968. Goliath is the largest American crocodile in the state, though Allen admits there are several bigger, mixed-breed gators elsewhere.

He tries to get Goliath to snap his jaws by prodding him with a stick, but the big croc is not in a cooperative mood today. He is hunkered under a thatched-roof tiki hut with nine gator skulls—his imagined trophies—on a railing.

"I just thought of a neat sign to put there: Who's Next?" Allen says, smiling.

He runs the state alligator egg collection program for the state's gator farmers. The year 2004 was a record one for egg collection—four thousand were collected. Eggs are brought initially to Gatorama and put in one of nine sixteen-foot-diameter concrete "grow-out" houses. They are later allocated to gator farmers under a quota system.

Gatorama also has several dozen uninvited guests—black vultures that often scamper atop the houses and get the gators excited, causing them to scrape and scar their skin.

"About your vultures . . . ," a visitor begins to ask.

"They're not my vultures," Allen quickly replies. "They're God's vultures."

The best book about crocodiles ever written? That's easy. *Eyelids of Morning: The Mingled Destinies of Crocodiles and Men*, by Alistair Graham and Peter Beard, is a stunning piece of natural-history reporting. It's an account of Graham's three years of research on Kenya's Lake Rudolf, complemented by Beard's two-hundred-plus photos. Here's one of my favorite passages from the book:

> Medieval bestiaries depicted crocs as "hell-mouths," the portals of irrevocable, despicable bestiality. A crocodile is a consuming, ravenous, raging beast. A passage from Solinus goes: The Egyptians . . . account a crocodile a savage, and cruel murdering beast, as may appear by their hieroglyphics, for when they will decipher a mad man, they picture a crocodile, who being put from his desired prey by forcible resistance, he presently rageth against himself.

Think Goliath is big? He couldn't hold a candle to prehistoric crocs:

The real monsters are long dead—even the massive estuarine crocs are mere pebbleworms compared to some of their ancient relatives. For some of them, like *Dinosuchus neivensis*, the Terrible Crocodile, a 30-footer that sculled the swamps of Colombia 100 million years ago, a Nile croc would have been no more than a handy snack. But the biggest of them all was Phobosuchus, the Fearsome Crocodile, an almost unimaginable 45 feet of pure croc.

Alligators also deserve their day in the sun. The best book on gators I've run across is *A Social History of the American Alligator*, by Vaughn L. Glasgow, who expertly traces the gator's colorful lore and legend, from the Indians' reverence toward the animal to its appearance in B movies and its popularity as a roadside attraction. One chapter is titled "Alligator, Inc.," about the gator's use in business and advertising. The gator on the famous alligator shirt from Lacoste, later Izod/Lacoste,

Gatorland, U.S. 441, South Orlando.

Daytona Beach Shores.

was originally a crocodile. Responding to letters from people who knew a croc when they saw one, the company changed the croc to a gator on its clothing.

Florida's colorful legacy of roadside gator attractions dates to the late nineteenth century. According to Glasgow:

> The oldest is the St. Augustine Alligator Farm, founded in the 1890s. Datable postcards recall some of the stellar examples of the early twentieth century, such as Alligator Joe's (Miami) and the Jacksonville Alligator Farm (Jacksonville), the Tampa Alligator Farm (Sulphur Springs), Ross Allen's Reptile Institute (Silver Springs), and even the Musa Isle Indian Village (where Seminole gator wrestlers entertained the tourists).

Gatorama opened in 1957, eight years after Gatorland in South Orlando. The highlight of any gator roadside attraction is the feeding, and Gatorama is no exception. Several gators in the lake are part of the original 1957 stock; gators in captivity can live up to sixty-five to seventy years. Crocs and gators swim together; they are not natural enemies. "It's a myth they don't get along," Allen says.

Shows are held at 11:30 A.M. and 2:30 P.M. Monday through Saturday and 4:30 P.M. on Sunday. A sign on the railing warns: "Danger. Do Not Set Anything Here." Parents have been known to set their kids up there. Not smart. Allen lost half a finger to one of his crocs several years ago, when she unexpectedly spun her head around and took a bite as he was feeding her. "She just snapped it right off," Allen says nonchalantly. "Lot of people asked, 'You killed her, didn't you?' No. She was just doing what she does."

You definitely don't want to dangle your digits anywhere near an alligator or crocodile. Crocs bite down at three thousand pounds per square inch, "the strongest biting-down pressure of any animal known to man," Allen says.

He walks into a fenced-off gated platform, a bucket of chicken and pork ribs in his hand. Gatorama buys meat—often freezer-burned or past its expiration date—from a wholesaler in Pompano. There are a lot of hungry mouths to feed here; Gatorama goes through sixteen thousand pounds of meat a month.

"You want to watch where you put your hands here," he tells me. As if on cue, a croc leaps half out of the water. Another smacks against the platform, jarring it. This is going to be fun.

Cameras click as Allen dangles huge slabs of ribs above the water. The questions come fast and furious. Many revolve around the differences between alligators and crocodiles. Alligators are blackish in color, not the mythical green. Crocs are more of a brown-tan. Gators are easily frightened and avoid confrontation; crocs tend to be more aggressive and are not intimidated. Gators have tongues; crocs do not. Gators can withstand cooler temperatures. Gators' eyes are set on top of the head; croc eyes are set in the head. Crocs need to eat just once every eighteen days under normal, 85-to-90-degree conditions.

Some of the questions are smarter than others. Visitors, noticing the beady eyes in the water, will ask where the live gators are. A woman once asked if the chicken fed to the gators was organic. She was from—big surprise—California.

Gatorama, Palmdale.

Honk if You Like the Church Service

Christmas Day, Daytona Beach, and church is about to begin. The two-hundred-plus people at the 10:30 A.M. service patiently wait in their seats. Some skim through the Sunday paper sports section or comics. Others make a few last-minute phone calls on their cell phones. A few pet or pamper their dogs, which have guessed by now where they are and behave accordingly.

Wait a minute—dogs, cell phones, and newspapers in church? "Good morning and Merry Christmas," Larry Deitch, minister of this unusual flock, begins. He announces that there's been a power outage and he hopes service will be restored soon. "The offices do not work; the phones do not work. Friendship Hall is dark. So far it has not affected our worship service."

Deitch says we are all to be commended for being in church on the Lord's Day, but the

Rev. Larry Deitch of Drive-In Christian Church.

53

Drive-In Christian Church, 3140 South Atlantic Avenue (Route AIA), Daytona Beach Shores.

DRIVE-IN CHRISTIAN C U CH

CHRISTMAS EVE SERVICE 7PM
SUNDAY WORSHIP 830 10AM
SUNDAY SCHOOL 945 AM

"special saints," he adds, are those who will be here next Sunday: New Year's Day.

There is a chorus of car horns. Deitch, standing behind a purple-cloth-draped, red-poinsettia-decorated railing, smiles. The honking horns come as high praise. His parishioners, sitting in their SUVs and pickup trucks, are faithful followers of the Drive-In Christian Church, on Route A1A in Daytona Beach Shores. It's the ultimate in worship convenience: You never have to leave your car, you can nod off without anyone noticing, and you don't have to subject yourself to Fred, your next-door neighbor, and his off-key singing.

"This is our third service in fourteen hours," continues Deitch, standing on a second-floor balcony. There were also an 8:30 A.M. service and a Christmas Eve service. "There are many people who made it possible, including," he says with a smile, "our dueling keyboardists. Will you help me thank them?"

A Hallelujah chorus of horns follows.

The Drive-In Christian Church is located at the site of the former Neptune Drive-In Theatre, which opened in 1932. The speaker posts are still in the ground, but the speakers are long gone; you listen to services on 680 AM or 88.5 FM. The first service was held in 1953; it was then called the South Peninsula Drive-In Church Service.

Glen Murdock, the first minister, apparently had a hard time convincing the central church of going the drive-in route. "The church board told him, 'That's the stupidest idea we've ever heard,'" Deitch says. "But he saw the potential to minister to the tourists."

The first service was held on May 26, 1953. About two hundred people showed up. The first offering: $80. Five years later, Paramount, the theater's owner, sold the twelve-acre property to the church for $120,000.

"We have developers offering to buy our property all the time," Deitch says. "The last offer was $30 million, and they offered to build another church somewhere else."

Drive-in speaker posts at Drive-In Christian Church.

No wonder; the church is located directly across from the ocean. Services are held at 8:30 and 10 A.M. Sundays. You drive through one of the two former drive-in theater gate houses and pick up a program, a miniature host, a cup of grape juice, and a Birch's Orange Candy Drop.

"Our purpose is to spread the Good News to every person, including tourists, the physically challenged, families with children and others looking for a unique way to worship," explains Deitch, minister since 1995.

The church is affiliated with the Christian Churches (Disciples of Christ). The national office is in Indianapolis, the regional office in Orlando. The drive-in church's website, driveinchurch.net, shows pictures of all church personnel, from Deitch, pianist Doug Wise, and organist Rosalie Hovencamp to maintenance men Frank Parker and Frank Mormur.

It's 66 degrees and raining lightly on this Christmas Day. We all join in to sing "Joy to the World," which is followed by a joyous round of car horns. You don't even have to leave your car to make a donation; men walk up and down the rows with large, green purses.

This is no solemn, hushed church service; Deitch keeps things informal, leavening the serious message with a sense of humor.

"The theme for this Christmas morning, if you haven't guessed it already, is wishing—wishing our power holds out for another fifteen minutes. Wishing you who are gathered here today have a wonderful day, a wonderful week, a wonderful life.

"There are a lot of wishes that go unfulfilled on Christmas Day," he continues. "I was expecting a Porsche under the tree. I didn't get it." He turns somber for a moment. "A lot of children are wishing for a meal today, and they will not get it. Our lives are chock full of wishes and dreams. If you're a wisher, the future is always filled with hope."

Along the way, he manages to weave in a Geico "I just saved a bunch of money on my car insurance" line. Naturally, someone honks in appreciation.

"Don't be afraid," he finishes. "God loves you."

A chorus sings "Silent Night." Deitch gives his benediction, slides the church doors closed, and the cars start rolling out of the yard.

"I used to come here years ago," says church member J. R. Stewart, standing outside. "I wore my bathing suit under my clothes. We would go to church, then right to the beach. That was eight years ago. Now I'm an usher." The drive-in church, he adds, is particularly attractive to pet owners. They can bring Fido or Fifi; the staff hands out dog biscuits.

The spiritual roadside in Miami.

Inside the church building, Deitch tells me, "Where you're sitting right now was where the screen was." The screen actually stayed up after services started back in 1953. The lease stipulated that movies had to be shown for at least three years after the purchase, so the drive-in church found itself a movie operator. The low-slung white building in the middle of the field was the old snack bar. The church has 1,100 members. About 825 of them are year-round residents; the rest are tourists and "snowbirds" from up north.

In twelve years, Deitch has had to preach inside only once. "There wasn't snow or rain or anything else," he says. "It was because of the wind."

He transferred here from a church in Akron, Ohio. His daughter's reaction to the move? "Great! Spring break at home."

Now sixty, Deitch figures to stay here until he retires. "Then it's, 'Do you want fries with that?'" he says, laughing.

He recently received a phone call from a congregation in Minnesota looking for a pastor.

"I said, 'It's February and the temperature is 74.' He said, 'Never mind.'"

Highway 441/27, Fruitland Park.

Put a Smile on Your FACE

In Florida, it seems as if everywhere you look there's a mural, large or small, elaborate or simple, painted on the side of a building or wall.

A drive down any of Miami's main drags, such as N.W. 36th Street or Miami Avenue, reveals scores of painted scenes, slogans, and messages on the side of restaurants, bars, clubs, markets, and stores. Lake Placid, in south-central Florida, describes itself as the "Town of Murals."

Mural-spotting can be a challenge; because this particularly vivid form of roadside art is often on the side or back of a building, murals are easy to miss. I was driving—aimlessly, as usual—through Tallahassee when I noticed a striking mural on the side of what turned out to be a homeless shelter. About twenty children and teens, all with hopeful expressions, are depicted against a landscape of green fields and blue skies. A message ambles across the top of the scene: "Alone All Alone Nobody Can Make It There Alone."

"It's from a Maya Angelou poem," said Jill Harper, founder-director of the Florida Arts and Community Enrichment (FACE) program.

Fifteen years ago, Harper, the wife of one of the city's more prominent attorneys, started volunteering at a local elementary school. She realized the importance of after-school programs for urban youth and founded FACE in 1991. "I saw the need for someone to work in a non-school environment with these children," she told the *Tallahassee Demo-*

crat. "The bare necessities of life are not enough. The arts can change and enrich the lives of young people."

FACE is "interdisciplinary—it involves all the arts," Harper said in a documentary, *A Project on 4th and Macomb*, produced and directed by Alex Banks and Nick Schwartz. Another goal, she added, "is to let the community know how much talent exist in the kids."

The first FACE programs were in African dancing and drumming, but as Harper read more and more about murals, she decided they should be a key part of FACE's mission. The first FACE mural, consisting of self-portraits of the children who participated, appeared on a grocery store in the city's Frenchtown section. "FACE represents the minds

The Shelter, 480 West Tennessee Street, Tallahassee.

of many different people, who try to reach higher than a hundred-foot steeple," one student said. "People unashamed of who they are and showing it proudly through the forms of their art."

The program's biggest project came in the form of the homeless shelter mural. The shelter, which provides "free, unconditional and unlimited accommodations" to 120 to 150 guests every night, was born from tragedy. In the winter of 1986, several men froze to death on the streets of Tallahassee. First Presbyterian Church opened a makeshift shelter in its basement, later moving it to the church nursery. The next winter, the program, by then known as the Tallahassee Cold Nights Shelter, had outgrown its space. Cold Nights Shelter was established as a nonprofit cor-

Another Shelter mural.

poration, but its future seemed tenuous, and the shelter was moved from site to site. Finally, in the spring of 1991, the shelter found a permanent home—rented storefronts on West Tennessee Street. It opened its doors on November 24, 1991, and has been open ever since.

In 1993, the shelter, with city and county funds, bought the building and embarked on a $154,000 renovation project, which included a new dining and day room, air-conditioning, and separate quarters for families. Information and referral services, GED and life-skills classes, legal services, health testing, and mental health outreach and treatment soon followed. The shelter now serves some twenty-five hundred guests a year; there are sixty beds for men and thirty for women and children. Guests receive free lodging, meals, showers, and laundry services, "providing they are willing to make a good faith effort to follow our policies and procedures," according to the mission statement.

Executive director Mel Eby is no mere figurehead; he spends 70 percent of his day on crisis intervention and counseling sessions. "He's a great guy," Harper said. "And quite a character."

Florida State University visiting professor Linda Hall helped Harper with the mural, which took just three days to paint. Forty local kids were brought in at different times to help. The seven- to ten-year-olds worked on the bottom, eleven- to fourteen-year-olds on the middle portion, and older teens on the upper reaches. The kids who helped paint the shelter mural were told to envision their idea of a home and draw it. The mural shows them holding homes above their heads—big homes, small homes, squarish homes, and rounded homes. The mural was originally

Palatka.

Miami.

Lake Placid.

Jacksonville.

Caloosa Cove.

painted in 1994; when it was repainted, the Twin Towers were added in the background.

If you decide to check out the mural, also walk around to the other side of the building, where you'll find another mural, this one painted by artist Mark Messersmith and others. To date, Harper and her youthful charges and artist friends have painted twenty-three murals at various spots around the city, including the city bus station, the police department, Winthrop Park, Odyssey Science Center, and Ebony Gardens Community Center. One mural shows a lush, green park; a bright, smiling sun; an adult and two children walking hand-in-hand down a path; and the words "And in the End, the Love You Take Is Equal to the Love You Make," echoing the Beatles. A FACE mural along once-gray walls inside the University Center at Florida State University is a vivid splash of greenery, hills, birds, and waterfalls. A mural of prehistoric Florida adorns the outdoor mezzanine at the Museum of Florida History in Tallahassee.

Other artists and musicians have volunteered their time to FACE, including Messersmith, sculptor O. L. Samuels, singer Velma Frye, and musician Charles Atkins. Atkins and several dozen children involved in the FACE program recorded a song called "Shine," which has become the group's anthem:

Let your life shine
Put a smile on your face

Shine when you're happy
Shine when you're glad
Shine when you feel like the world has made you mad
Shine all around you and everywhere you go
Shine and be happy because Jesus loves you so.

Not only has FACE unlocked artistic talent, but it has also elevated self-esteem, even found kids jobs. "FACE gave me motivation," one seventeen-year-old told the Tallahassee Democrat. He was promoted to manager of a fast-food restaurant after only four months on the job. "I've seen it turn people completely around," he said.

FACE continues to brighten children's lives as well as the landscape of the state capital. Harper hopes more murals will be painted around town and that her kids will use the art and life lessons they learned in FACE later on.

"The greatest gift," she said, "is the gift of art."

Midget Mountain

Florida is flatter than a roadkilled pancake, so it should come as no surprise that the Sunshine State has the lowest highpoint among the fifty states. Lower than Louisiana, high point 535 feet; lower than Mississippi, 806 feet; lower than Rhode Island, 812 feet. Lower, for goodness sake, than even Delaware, whose highest point, Ebright Azimuth, is 448 feet above sea level.

Britton Hill, several miles from the Alabama border in Walton County, is Florida's high point, at the somewhat-less-than-nosebleed-producing height of 345 feet.

You can have Mauna Kea, at 13,796 feet, the highpoint in Hawaii; Mount McKinley, Alaska's high point at 20,320; or Mount Whitney, California's highest spot at 14,494 feet. For beauty and serenity, I'd take Britton Hill. And unlike the previous three, you can drive right to the top.

The picnic grove–like spot along County Road 187 is ringed by pines and offers sweeping views of the surrounding countryside. Benches circle a granite marker. There are restrooms and a rack where you can pick up helpful brochures from the Highpointers Club (highpointers.org).

Mostly, though, there's a whole lot of peace and quiet.

Florida's highest point is located in Lakewood, an unincorporated hamlet in northwest Walton County. Former major league baseball commissioner Bill White was born here. Jacqueline Cochran, an aviator and founder of a perfume company, spent part of her childhood here. In 1953, she became the first woman to break the sound barrier.

Pine trees put Lakewood on the map. Britton Hill is named after William "Will" Britton, a timber baron from North Carolina who bought a lumber company in Florala, Alabama, and moved it three miles east, naming the site Lakewood. At one time, the bustling town contained 101 buildings, including a Victorian hotel, commissary, mercantile store, train depot, and sawmill. The floors of Grand Central Station and the Waldorf-Astoria Hotel, among other buildings, were made of longleaf pine from Lakewood. But Britton's death in 1909, according to an account in a local newspaper, "was the first in a series of events that led to the slow decline of the company and eventually Lakewood itself."

The town made a comeback of sorts in 1956, when a survey revealed it to be the state's highest point, not Crestview, Lake Wales, or Laurel Hill, as officials in those towns claimed. Brochures trumpeted Lakewood's new claim to fame.

Britton Hill marker, County Road 187, Lakewood.

Islamorada.

Bithlo.

Florida City.

But being the lowest high point in America is not something you can make a public relations mountain out of. Stories started to poke fun at this distant corner of Florida. A 1982 AP story described Lakewood's "midget mountain," and visitors showed up in mountain gear to scale the less-than-forbidding heights.

The furor came and went. Today Britton Hill remains what it has always been: a beautiful, if seriously out-of-the-way spot.

"To enjoy the experience safely, please make certain your level of experience and preparation is equal to the route you select," reads the Highpointers Club brochure. "Weather, season, road and access, party numbers, and individual experience and physical condition are all variables for which only you can accept responsibility."

You don't have to worry about any of that to scale the heights of Britton Hill. It's an easy ride down a winding country road; look for signs along Highway 331, which runs north from DeFuniak Springs to Florala and the Alabama state line.

Stand in front of the marker and get your picture taken. Then just stay a while to breathe in the fresh air, stunning views, and silence. It's the highest spot in Florida. It may well be the quietest, too.

You Will Be Seeing Unusual Accomplishment

Seventy years after Florida's oddest tourist attraction was built, the question remains: How did he do it?

How did Edward Leedskalnin, a diminutive, frail, and often sickly Latvian immigrant, build his unlikely rock wonderland, which he named Coral Castle, along U.S. 1 in Homestead?

How did Leedskalnin, who had worked his way across the country as a mason, logger, and ranchhand before settling in Florida City, move tons of coral rock to the ten-acre plot of land he had purchased in 1936? Was it really just a matter of Leedskalnin using only hand tools to cut and move huge blocks of coral, as coralcastle.com suggests?

> People would look at me, all five foot and 100 pounds, and almost laugh. I hated it when asked how I moved and carved such pieces. Everyone knows if you understand the principles of weight and balance as were used in Egypt to build the pyramids, you can move the world.

That's Eddie, or someone impersonating Eddie, on the Coral Castle audio tour. The monolithic-looking complex, darkly mysterious and enchanting at the same time, is the most unlikely tourist attraction on U.S. 1 and maybe in all of Florida. Its setting—just north of Homestead center, on a ragged stretch of highway—makes it all the more surreal.

About sixty thousand people visit Coral Castle every year, drawn by the oddball zaniness and its back story. Coral Castle is an engineering feat that may rival the building of the pyramids; it is also a story of love gone bad. In Latvia, Leedskalnin was engaged to a girl, Agnes Scuffs. He called her "Sweet Sixteen," for her age. But Agnes changed her mind at the last moment.

Cupid's arrow found its mark. My Agnes was ten years younger, but I was smitten by her charm. I failed to see the danger. The night before our wedding she left me, claiming I was too old and poor.

Crushed by her rejection, he emigrated to the United States and began a cross-country journey that landed him in Florida City. In 1923, he bought an acre of land for $12 and started building a rock garden.

Coral Castle, 28655 South Dixie Highway (U.S. 1), Homestead.

Coral Castle original admission marker.

My neighbors' curiosity got the best of me and soon I was giving tours of Eden for ten cents. Life was good and I was happy until civilization started moving in around me.

But developers had sensed potential in South Florida, even in the 1930s, and plans were made to build a subdivision near his home. Leedskalnin craved privacy, so he picked up and moved a few miles north, buying a ten-acre plot in Homestead. Over the next fifteen years, from 1936 to 1951, he completed his remarkable structure, a monument to his undying love for the no-longer-sweet Agnes.

He built a nine-ton gate, balanced on ball bearings, that moved at the touch of a finger; eleven half-ton chairs; a nearly fifty-foot-high, thirty-ton obelisk; a sixty-thousand-pound stone along the north wall; and other objects.

Locals remember an old Republic truck carting rock from Florida City to Homestead, but no one, according to the Coral Castle website, ever saw Leedskalnin loading or unloading it. He worked at night by lantern light. The castle's high walls discouraged snoops and busybodies.

When asked how he moved the rock, Leedskalnin replied only that "he knew the laws of weight and leverage well," according to Coral Castle's official history. "There is no record of anyone observing Ed carving in Florida City or Homestead. He has baffled engineers and scientists! People have compared Ed's secret method of construction to Stonehenge and the Great Pyramids."

So what did he do, levitate the rocks? Well, some believe so. According to an article in *Fate* magazine, "some teenagers spying on him one evening claimed they saw him float coral blocks through the air like hydrogen balloons."

It gets better. A pilot for a New Zealand airline offered a complicated, and kooky, explanation. Coral Castle, he said, was ideally situated to create "the geometric harmonics necessary for the manipulation of anti-gravity."

The Gate and Feast of Love Table at Coral Castle.

Coral Castle, he said, tapped into a worldwide power grid that had been set up "between some groups on this planet and UFOs."

"I have discovered the secrets of the pyramids, and have found out how the Egyptians and the ancient builders in Peru, Yucatan and Asia, with only primitive tools, raised and set in place blocks of stone weighing many tons!" Leedskalnin once exulted.

Yes, but the Egyptians and others had help; Eddie built Coral Castle by himself.

A stargazer, he carved Mars, Saturn, and a crescent moon out of massive rock. "I used to sit in that moon and wave at cars on Route 1," he says on the tape.

A photograph from the time reveals a square-jawed, stern-looking man. He carved rock beds, a three-ton rocking chair, a cement-lined tub, and a heart-shaped, two-and-a-half-ton Feast of Love table listed in *Ripley's Believe It or Not* as the world's largest Valentine. He built a Throne Room with massive chairs. The only chair that

Ron Jon's, North Atlantic Avenue, Cocoa Beach.

Xanadu, Highway 192, Kissimmee.

WonderWorks, International Drive, Orlando.

was uncomfortable was the one designed for his future mother-in-law; he wanted to keep her visits short.

He built a Repentance Corner "for when my Sweet Sixteen sasses me back," although by that time Agnes Scuffs had long since left him. Sixteen steps ("perhaps 16 is on my mind too much") led upstairs. He lived alone. He kept his life savings, $3,500, in an old tripod he used as a radio stand.

He earned the money giving 10-cent, and later 25-cent, tours of his castle. In December 1961, he put up a sign out front reading, "Going to the Hospital," and checked into Jackson Memorial in Miami. Three days later, on December 7, he died in his sleep at the age of sixty-four.

> Three days later I passed on to another life, but I can still look down and see my beloved rock garden, which passed on to my nephew Harry in Detroit. He didn't want it, so a man in Chicago bought it to operate as a tourist attraction. He sold it in 1980 to his cousin.

Doris Wishman, director of such sixties exploitation shockers as *Bad Girls Go to Hell* and *Let Me Die a Woman*, filmed her 1963 cult hit *Nude on the Moon* at Coral Castle. Billy Idol wrote a song, "Sweet Sixteen,"

Miami.

inspired by a visit here. Coral Castle was added to the National Register of Historic Places in 1984.

> As a tourist attraction. I like to think Coral Castle is an attraction for the mind. It will cause you to think and dream. Did I really do this with my physical strength alone? With only a fourth-grade education, was I really capable of understanding the universe?
>
> When you go into the gift shop don't forget to buy the four-color book which tells the story of Coral Castle. It has been my extreme pleasure to have you here today. Please tell a friend of your remarkable discovery. So long.

Coral Castle is open seven days a week, year-round. A sign on one section of wall reads: "You Will Be Seeing Unusual Accomplishment." The owners of Coral Castle say it's "one of the world's most remarkable" achievements. "The only other tribute that can compare to the Coral Castle is the Taj Mahal."

That's a bit much. Roadsideamerica.com calls Coral Castle "an impressive display of obsessive, unrequited love."

That's more like it. But the question remains: How did little Eddie do it? Seventy years later, we're still searching for an answer.

Leesburg.

Sasquatch of the South

Dave Shealy—goateed, bare chested, baseball cap turned backward—is single-handedly trying to drag a hot tub across the muck and mire of his yard when I show up. It's a steamy day in the Everglades, which admittedly is like saying it rains a lot in Seattle or New Jersey has an image problem.

Shealy and I coerce the massive tub into his pickup truck, then the two of us team up to rig a PVC-pipe railing to the side of the boat he's about to take on a three-week shrimp-fishing trip. Shealy excuses himself to take a shower, and I sit on the outside porch of his modest home at Trail Lakes Campground in Ochopee, basking in the heat and humidity as if it were part of a cure. It is below freezing back home, after all.

Shealy returns, dish of spaghetti and Pepsi in hand. It is time to talk

Dave Shealy of Skunk Ape Research Headquarters, 40904 Tamiami Trail East (Highway 41), Ochopee.

Entrance to Skunk Ape Research Headquarters and a friendly panther on the grounds.

of myths and monsters, of local lore and legend. It is time to talk about the skunk ape.

"We got quite the little roadside attraction going here," he says, smiling, at the warehouse-like building that houses his Skunk Ape Research Headquarters.

Forget that Skunk Ape Headquarters basically consists of a gift shop—gator heads and teeth, maps, bottled water—and a zoo complete with anacondas, pythons, king snakes, parrots, and the odd duck or two. Forget that Ochopee, about halfway between Fort Myers and Miami, is in the middle of nowhere, a faint flicker of a town in the primordial vastness that is the Everglades.

Thousands of tourists manage to find the place every year, drawn by tales of a half man, half beast, and a foul-smelling one at that. The skunk ape, the locals call it, although Shealy is far more convinced of its existence than anyone else.

"I've seen it three times," he says matter-of-factly. "Once, when I was ten, right back there." He nods toward the wilderness at the campground's fringe, part forest, part swamp, all part of the Big Cypress National Preserve. "My brother and I ran like hell out of the woods."

The term "skunk ape" was coined by Shealy's dad, Jack, in the 1960s, when he and friend Ray Wooten "caught a whiff of the monster," according to an hourlong documentary by Nate Martin, *The Ochopee Skunk Ape*. Jack Shealy led a band of researchers into the Fakahatchee Strand, a swatch of Big Cypress where most of the sightings have been made, but the expedition yielded no concrete evidence of the beast.

Today his son has taken up the skunk ape crusade, willingly talking up the Sasquatch of the Sunshine State when he is not attending to the aches and pains that come from running a campground.

"Campground?" Shealy says at one point in the movie. "It's Campground Hell. It's tough owning a campground, man. You've got to be the cop, you've got to be the bookkeeper, you've got to be the hostess with the most-est, and I ain't any of that shit."

The movie, by turns hokey, half-baked, and enormously entertaining, describes Shealy as "an internationally renowned crypto-zoologist" and "Florida's forerunner in the field of skunk ape research." Admittedly, it's a one-man field. Shealy has appeared on *Unsolved Mysteries*, *The Daily Show* with Jon Stewart, and other shows, but he's been a lone voice crying out in this wilderness.

The second time he saw the skunk ape, he was fourteen. He was with friends on a weeklong dune-buggy safari. "We were pretty out there," he says, sitting on his patio. One morning, while walking in the bush, he spotted "a large set of tracks, barefooted tracks. We were eighteen to twenty miles from anywhere. A lot of people made a big joke out of it."

They still do. "It's a joke," a waitress at a nearby restaurant told the *Miami Herald*. "It's one of them in a monkey suit."

More than a few old-timers believe *something* is out there, though not necessarily a skunk ape. A clerk at the Glades Haven Grocery Store told the *Herald* that men return from hunting trips to the swamp shaken. "You hear bloodcurdling screams, things that you can't describe," she said.

In the documentary, Burl Thompson, an airboat tour guide, says he spotted a skunk ape in the late sixties, early seventies. "I saw this—I thought it was a man, walking way up the road. I thought it was someone on a buggy broke down. A man, a good seven feet tall, walked kind of stiff-legged. I got up there pretty close. He turned. He saw me and he made a turn off the road."

Local Mike Kelly says he spotted the beast, and crabber "Barnacle Bill" thinks he might have. Another local, Jack Labin, had this to say: "Usually you heard the words 'skunk ape' and you heard the words 'Dave Shealy' and you had to determine which was which, you know?"

Shealy has played the skunk ape to maximum camp effect. He put on a monkey suit to reenact the skunk ape for the TV show *Unsolved Mysteries*. In a scene in Martin's documentary, he walks up to a fence, spots a few strands of hair, takes a whiff, and pronounces, "That's a skunk ape."

He comes across as an Everglades Crocodile Dundee in the movie, wearing a bushman hat, camouflage pants, and cutoff shirt. There's Dave in his house, bag of pretzels by his side. There's a photo of Dave as a freckle-faced kid. There's Dave on his John Deere, Dave in his white pickup with a skull-and-crossbones license plate, out looking for skunk ape. At one point, he "finds" a sixteen-inch track on the ground. "Tracks everywhere; this place is covered with tracks," he proclaims.

Deerland.

Caloosa Cove.

The video is available for $20 at Skunk Ape Research Headquarters. In it, he tells viewers what they need to mount their own skunk ape expedition. A ladder stand is "a must for somebody wanting to come to the Everglades and hunt skunk apes." He has spent a month or more perched on his twenty-foot-high ladder stand, hoping to spot the elusive animal.

In the movie, he talks about obtaining "classified state wildlife records from a secret contact inside the park system," which reveal the existence of an "unknown primate species" living in the Everglades thirty-odd years ago.

The skunk ape's diet is said to include palmetto berries, sawgrass, and possibly alligator and deer, but it fancies one food most of all: lima beans, cooked or uncooked. There's Dave in a local store, shopping for lima beans. There's Dave scattering lima beans on the ground.

"The downside of the beans is that if the skunk ape is anywhere in the vicinity, he'll be passing gas; it'll be double times as bad," he says helpfully. "So when you're using the beanset, after it gets hit, get out of the woods."

Beans apparently were the cause of one of the first alleged sightings, in 1963. Five hunters in a cabin were cooking a pot of beans and play-

Gainesville.

Roadside cows.

ing cards when a skunk ape, drawn by the smell, leaned over too far on a tree limb and came crashing through the cabin roof. "Everyone freaked," Dave says. Before the hunters could draw their guns, the ape busted out. "True story," Dave promises.

On his campground porch, he says the Glades were once rife with drug smugglers. "Kind of got caught up in that," he admits. He was arrested in 1989 for possession of thirty thousand pounds of pot and spent three years in federal prison. He once encountered some coke smugglers who were determined to find and shoot the skunk ape. They were busted for possession last year instead.

Shealy has scaled back his skunk ape forays in recent years; the campground demands more and more of his time. Every June, though, he holds his Skunk Ape Festival, with live entertainment and bands. Six hundred or so people pack the yard.

"I hold it the absolute worst time of year; the mosquitoes are the worst," he admits. "Only the true believers are here at that time."

He is mum about his third skunk ape sighting, several years ago. "I'm under contract for that particular sighting, so I can't tell you about that. I have a seven-minute video; that's all I can tell you." He says the video will be the basis of a one-hour prime-time television special.

What about the skeptics? "It's people who have never been here before, who've never spent time in the Everglades, people who are telling me what's in my backyard," he says. Or it's Bigfoot believers who say an ape man can't exist in Florida "and have written some really nasty things about me. I don't let it bother me too much."

He admits he's waging a one-man battle. "When you're winning, everyone's on your side. In all the years I've done this, I really haven't made any money." Why does he keep doing it? "I've done it long enough, I really can't quit."

The movie's most engaging character is Floyd Brown, a crusty old local. "There is—something, for sure there is something out there," Brown says in one entertaining passage. "Without a doubt has been, has always been something. There is something, I don't know if it's a skunk ape, Bigfoot, or crow's foot or what."

The end credits announce: "No skunk apes were harmed during the filming of this movie."

The soundtrack, on a second disk, is surprisingly good, including "Way Down South," "In the Everglades," and other hearty helpings of swamp rock. One of the more memorable tunes is Rubee Jawbotik's "Can It Be?" Call it Everglades rap with a touch of reggae and what I could have sworn was a whiff of Gerry and the Pacemakers.

> Can it be?
> An unsolved mystery
> going down in Ochopee
> Can it be?
> I'll guess we'll wait and see.

Muffler Men

Highway 441 zigs and zags its way through Miami and Fort Lauderdale, often changing course (pay attention!) and streets as it heads north toward West Palm. It's a commerce-crazy highway, jammed with gas stations, convenience stores, fast-food restaurants, and probably more auto repair and body shops, transmission places, and car dealerships than any other highway in the country.

Somehow, in the midst of this souped-up reminder of our love affair with the automobile, two muffler shops on 441—at 10051 N.W. 7th Avenue in Miami and 4950 Highway 7/441 in Hollywood—stand out.

"He's got a couple loose screws," Steve Pearl is saying inside the Miami Mad Hatter Muffler. "He's got a *sick* mind." Pearl is not talking about a wacko customer or some itinerant oddball, but his business partner. The guy with the sick mind—in the same breath, Pearl calls him creative—is Kevin Doyle, the other half of Mad Hatter Muffler. They each install mufflers in one of the two shops. Both can tell you everything you ever wanted to know about catalytic converters and Flowmaster mufflers. Both can do the occasional nonmuffler job, like the horse trailer with a busted door that pulled in one day. But Doyle turns everyday mufflers into something fun and fanciful; he makes eye-catching art out of this most ordinary of essential car parts.

Just stop at either shop. In front of each is a menagerie of creatures—dogs, snakes, giraffes, alligators, rabbits, and horses, among others. Mufflers make up their bodies, their legs are often pipes, their tongues flanges, their feet muffler brackets, and so on. Whatever mufflers and

Red, white, and blue muffler man at Mad Hatter.

Steve Pearl at Mad Hatter, 10051 N.W. 7th Avenue, Miami.

spare parts are around, Kevin fashions them into his highway folk art.

But don't call it that. A local college teacher told Kevin she brings her students to the Hollywood shop because it's a local example of folk art. His reaction? "Folk art? It's just fun."

He may be Miami's least pretentious artist. You want his artwork, just drive to the Hollywood shop and speak to Kevin; he's the guy with the long hair and gray-flecked beard welding pipe in the garage bay. Tell him what you're looking for; it'll be ready in a week or two, maybe longer, depending on business.

It helps to provide basic information, like your name. Not long ago, a guy pulled up in a

Kevin Doyle at Mad Hatter, 4950 Highway 7/441, Hollywood.

fancy convertible and told the artist he wanted a rabbit, duck, and several other creatures. How much would it cost? Kevin did some quick calculation and told him $1,200. The guy pulled out a wad of bills, counted out $1,200, handed it to Kevin, and drove away. Ten minutes later, he returned and told the muffler man, "I should give you my name and phone number."

Kevin isn't sure how he went from muffler man to artist. Born in Trenton, New Jersey, he moved with his family to the Miami area when he was two. A graduate of Norland High School, he started making pieces on a whim when he opened the Miami shop in 1981. But he didn't start selling them until the Hollywood shop opened about ten years later. A woman drove up one day in a luxury sedan and told Kevin she wanted to buy a muffler giraffe he had made. He told her it wasn't for sale. More people stopped by, and pretty soon Kevin changed his mind.

"It's not a full-time job," he says of his art. "If it was, they wouldn't have whimsical faces; they'd have serious faces. They have to be goofy—goofy sells."

"We do mufflers; he fools around," Steve cracks.

They've known each other for thirty years. Kevin and his father-in-law, Pete Lynn, started fixing mufflers at Mad Hatter locations in Dade and Broward in the early 1980s. Steve worked for them for a while, got a job elsewhere, came back to work at the Miami shop, left to work for a motor home company, and returned a third time, this time as Kevin's partner.

"That's his doodling," Steve says. "Instead of drawing, he uses metal. He's done some creative stuff—a cow with tits, a turkey, and a six-foot duck."

You'd think no one would possibly object to adorable dogs, ducks, cats, rabbits, even cows with tits. But the state did. No sooner had Kevin installed Fred, an eight-foot-high muffler-headed man, along the curb of the Miami shop than someone from the Department of Transportation paid a visit. He took some snapshots, then, according to the *Miami Herald*, slapped a bright orange sticker on an unsuspecting Fred. Kevin learned he was in violation of Chapter 337.406 of the state code, which prohibits the obstruction of any right-of-way. Pete Lynn threatened to chain himself to Fred in protest. His son-in-law faced a fine and more trouble than it was worth. Fred was moved away from the highway.

"I don't know why they called him a hazard," says Steve, ever sarcastic. "He never hit anybody."

To this day, Fred's creator doesn't understand all the fuss.

"If I'm driving down the highway and I have the option of hitting a tin man or hitting a pole, I'm going for the tin man," Kevin says.

His display pieces are bolted to the ground, which didn't keep what we'll call the Muffler Man Highway Robbery of 2005 from happening. A hurricane late in the year knocked out power in the area; at night, the shop, normally lit by streetlight, was pitch black. In the middle of the night, the dastardly criminals struck. "They came by with a torch and saw and cut out the rabbit and dog," Kevin says with a smile. "The cops got a kick out of that. They asked if there was a reward."

The rabbit and dog have never been found, and no, there isn't a reward. What does a muffler rabbit fetch on the black market, anyway? Kevin's pieces generally sell for several hundred dollars or more; I own one of his muffler frogs, its PT Cruiser muffler body flanked by curved-pipe legs.

Dogs are the easiest animals to make and the most popular of Kevin's pieces. Some are spotted, like dalmatians, or big-eared, like chihuahuas. They come in different shapes, sizes, and colors; he's even made red, white, and blue "patriotic pooches." The most commonly used muffler is the 1996–97 Dodge truck muffler, which Kevin says has "the perfect shape for bending exhaust tubing around."

Tools of this artist's trade are few: torch, pipe bender, rubber hammer. Materials: mufflers, exhaust pipe, spray paint. You can flip through portfolios of Kevin's work at the Hollywood shop, where a sense of humor prevails. "We Do Not Charge Tax, We Collect It," reads one sign. "Please Pardon Our Appearance. We Have Been Renovating for 12 Years," says another. One portfolio is labeled "rabbits, horses and a hockey rat," another "muffler dogs," a third "misc. goofy muffler art pictures."

Schoolchildren are frequent visitors. Thank-you notes from one class trip are taped to the wall.

"Dear Mr. Doyle," reads one. "I like the animals you made for us. Your job is so fun. I like your job. Maybe I wish to be a Muffler. Michelle."

Kevin has donated pieces to local schools; he will donate a book-holding figure to a library. His patio is a museum of muffler men, women, and animals. There's a spectacular multicolored parrot, made from a catalytic converter, flanges, and pieces of pipe, swinging on a perch. A small elephant made from a catalytic converter from a Dodge truck and a muf-

Two joyous Muffler Men at Mad Hatter, Hollywood.

fler from a Ford truck. A turkey with eleven yellow-orange tail-feather pipes, with a Volvo muffler body, a chain for its wattle, muffler brackets for feet, and muffler heat shields for its wings.

"I looked at the muffler, said that's the body, there's the turkey," Steve explains.

One of his more elaborate works is a duo: a horse with 200 feet of chain-link hair and a miniature mustached cowboy, with washers for spurs, a disk rotor for a hat, a piece of pipe for his gun handle, and a catalytic converter air tube as the barrel. The horse and cowboy are $600. People have offered $300 for each separately. "No, no," Steve says. "They go together."

He seems amused by all the attention his pieces have received. They've been exhibited at galleries; they've made local and national news. Kevin just shrugs his shoulders. He does it for fun. For the Hol-

Port Richey.

Hollywood.

Americana on the road.

Panacea.

lywood St. Patrick's Day parade, he builds a float and packs it with all sorts of muffler creatures. And he throws a mean Fourth of July party at his modest lakeside home in Davie, entertaining up to 150 guests and shooting off $3,000 worth of fireworks.

The muffler man has made some three hundred pieces to date, and he'll create any animal you want. "Name an animal; I bet I can make it," he told one customer. Big mistake. "How about a meerkat?" she asked. His reaction: "What's a meerkat?" But his kids helped him out, and Steve made a meerkat.

After he finished the piece, the woman called and asked, "Does it look like a meerkat?"

"I think it has the essence of a meerkat," he told her, "or it's a regular cat with a bad hair day."

Beautiful Fruit, Beautiful People

The signs in front of the roadside market in Highway 27 in Leesburg burst with life, color, and fresh-picked fruit.

"Strawberries. 2 for 2. Just for You," announces a juicy-pink sign. "Eat Lots of Melons!" advises a greenish one. "Fruit Is Love and Compassion That's Never Out of Season," says a third, signed Dr. Fergie. One particularly vivid sign is a near-psychedelic swirl of peaches, bananas, and watermelon. "We Sell the Best and Junk the Rest!" trumpets another.

Signs are splashed along the road and clear across the parking lot fence; dozens more are stacked in rows out back. "Adam Ate the Apple; Jesus Paid the Price." And "Jesus. He Is the Real Thing."

The signs, painted in bright, nearly blinding colors, practically dared me to stop in. The roadside market, on an otherwise unremarkable stretch of highway, is the kind of place that grabs you by the collar—and proceeds to lavish a whole lot of love on you.

"Beautiful Fruit. Beautiful People," pronounces yet another sign.

How could I resist?

The man behind this Technicolor production is inside the open-air market, checking, as he does every morning, for overripe fruit. "People call this Dr. Fergie's Fruit and Color World," Donald Ferguson says. "This is the most colorful place in Florida."

It's hard to argue with that. Ferguson opened the market in 1982. His father, Hayward Ferguson, was a farmer in the Bahamas. Donald Ferguson emigrated to the United States when he was nineteen—"with less than

$10 in my pocket," he says. The family first settled in Fort Pierce and later moved to Leesburg, where the older Ferguson worked for a produce firm.

"He was an awesome worker. He was bad to the bone," Ferguson, now fifty-six, says of his dad, who bought land on Highway 44, opening a roadside market there in 1967. "He instilled in me the morals I needed to live. He said, 'America is the greatest country in the world.' He said, 'I didn't bring you to America to be a bum. There are already enough bums in America.' He said, 'Go into the fruit business.' I said, 'Daddy, I don't know anything about fruit.' He said, 'No matter how rich or poor you are, fruit is something everyone can enjoy.'"

Dr. Fergie's Fruit and Color World, Highway 27, Leesburg.

Donald "Dr. Fergie" Ferguson.

Ferguson took a business course at LSU in the early seventies, opening the Leesburg stand in 1982. "I learned in the course that the eyes are the gateway to the heart, and the heart is the source of desire," he explains.

His dream was to open a market that was exciting and beautiful. But Dr. Fergie's Fruit and Color World was not well received at first because of the color of the signs and the color of Ferguson's skin. "This town at the time was known as a redneck town," he says. "A black man was not treated well. There were people who were prejudiced dealing with you."

Some locals considered the market an eyesore and complained about the religious nature of some of the signs. The city cited him for various violations in 1982. In 1987, Ferguson spent $2,000 and two days to put thousands of plastic oranges in the oak tree out front. City officials didn't like that, either.

A visit by a vice president might have been the highlight and lowlight in the market's history. His father once told him, "Son, you always want to keep a clean market. You never know when the president of the United States will stop." The president never stopped, but Vice President Dan Quayle did. Ferguson heard the Quayles might be coming through town, so he put up signs reading, "Welcome Mr. and Mrs. Quayle. God Loves You. And We Do, Too." The Quayles did stop. "This is the most beautiful market I have ever seen," Marilyn Quayle told Ferguson.

But he paid a price for his celebrity. The next morning, he opened the market to find his watermelons sliced open, eggs broken, windows broken, and racial slurs written everywhere. "It was a complete mess," he says. Stuck in a watermelon was a knife and a note: "Nigger—This is going to happen to you."

Police were stationed at the market round the clock for six weeks; there were no further incidents.

Psychedelic fruit sign at Dr. Fergie's.

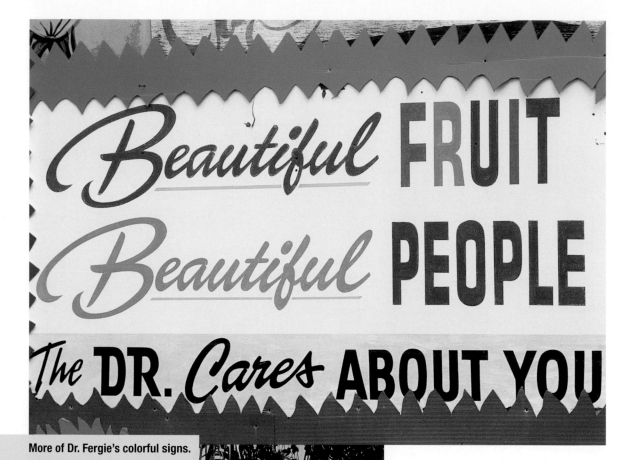

More of Dr. Fergie's colorful signs.

"I didn't give up," Ferguson says. "I have a saying: If you think you're right, you'll fight. If you're wrong, you'll get along."

Everything's cool now. Dr. Fergie even received a key to the city. Steven Tyler stopped by in 1991, but the Aerosmith lead singer might as well have been Steven Spielberg. "I had no idea who the guy was," Ferguson says. "It got crazy here."

The Highway 44 stand operated until 2001, when his father suffered a stroke. "He was eighty-five at the time. Still working, still working hard. He said, 'Leave me alone, let me keep working, I will die happy.'"

Hayward Ferguson passed away several years ago.

A customer is on the phone. "You want tomatoes on the pink side?" Ferguson asks. "No problem with that. You want your tomatoes on the pink side, I will take care of you, brother. You're dealing with a man who's been in this business for thirty-five years; he will do you no wrong."

"I'm as cool as a cucumber," he says a few minutes later. "I'm whatever way the wind blows."

He conducts much of his business in an open-air shed, decorated with newspaper clippings, photos of his parents, and various awards and certificates. In the eighties, there was an area out back called Gentle World. It was a place where you could sit down, chill out. He's thinking about bringing Gentle World back.

Dr. Fergie's prescription for a healthy life can be found on one sign: "Eat Fruits, Nuts and Vegetables Daily!"

"That's the only prescription I can write, because I can't give you Valium or Zanax," Ferguson says, laughing.

But he can give you fruit, and plenty of it. Fruit, he believes, is an ideal medium to convey his faith. "Fruit is very special because of the love I have for the Lord. Fruit and love go together."

Miami.

Clewiston.

St. Petersburg.

Make that fruit, love, and those loud, luscious signs.

"I love colors," the proprietor of Ferguson's Fruit and Color World says with a smile. "They used to call me the psychedelic kid in the Bahamas. I wore all-color shoes. I wore orange and red suits. I could never be in a place all black and white. Pastels I don't like. I've got to have color. Bright, beautiful colors."

Postscript: Sadly, Donald Ferguson died in a car accident in October 2005, a few weeks after I visited with him.

Signs, Signs

Signs promote businesses, list services, advertise specials, offer advice, and generally do everything they can to attract, entice, and beckon. There are millions of signs in Florida—I doubt any state has more—and part of the purpose of this book is to finally give them their due. Signs, as seen in the following pages, are often works of art. I don't mean museum-quality things of beauty. The signs here are often crudely lettered and hastily painted—but charmingly effective.

They can be put up along the side of the road, in front of businesses, atop storefronts—wherever they are apt to catch your eye and, with luck, a piece of your wallet. They don't have to be self-standing pieces of plywood or metal. They can take the form of murals; objects, such as a missile advertising an army surplus store; or words and messages splashed on the side of a wall.

Miami.

Signs in Miami.

Even a memorable store name is a sign in itself. How could you drive past Booty Shake Car Wash or Get Down Motors, both in Miami? How could you ignore Mr. Special in Miami or the Bead Chick in St. Augustine?

In Florida, Miami in particular, painted messages and murals on the fronts or sides of buildings reach their zenith. Miami is a nonstop roadside art gallery. Just drive up and down a commercial-crazy street like N.W. 7th Avenue in Miami. Look close; these works of art are not lit up in neon and bright lights. You might have to peer around the side of a building or focus on one facade in a long, colorful row of them.

On the side of one bar-restaurant on N.W. 7th Avenue, an artist has painted glittering stars and planets and the words, "Just Eat Fish & Live Longer." There is one owner who cared about beautifying an otherwise drab storefront and neighborhood and had a sense of style and humor besides.

Other signs are more direct. When you see a sign for Bubba's Supermarket, don't you want to stop in and see if there really is a Bubba around?

Miami.

More signs in Miami.

Or Nookie, the owner of Nookies 99 Store? Dollar stores are a dime a dozen, but who could resist this pitch, in front of a Hollywood bargain emporium: "Why Pay a Dollar When You Can Spend 97¢." There's a market in Ocala called Big Midget; what's that about?

Often, the more humble the storefront, the more bewitching the sign. On the side of a spare-looking restaurant on N.W. 66th Street in Miami is a handpainted grill, with sizzling ribs and chicken and the words "One Love Hot Grill."

Those of highbrow nature would consider this type of highway vernacular not worthy of the word *art*. Many of us who dig side-of-the-road color and whimsy would argue otherwise. Even the great American photographer Walker Evans, coauthor with James Agee of the classic *Let Us Now Praise Famous Men*, spent a lifetime on the lookout for memorable signs and storefronts, the more simple and direct, the better.

Take this 1936 sign, one of fifty reproduced in *Signs*, a book of Evans's work published by the J. Paul Getty Museum. Several words are mispelled, and punctuation is in short supply, but the message is unmistakable:

Truck Excursion Thursday July 2 1936 Truck Leave Lyse Cafe at 4 oclock going to Oak Grove and Union Town to Dine and Dance Come Follow the Crod to Brown's Come and Trucr with us Adm. 25¢

My favorite sign in the book is a 1936 Evans photo of a roadside market in Birmingham. Two sturdy-looking lads, watermelons held above their heads, stand outside. Around them are baskets of fruit and vegetables. The entire storefront is one marvelous Depression-era come-on. One sign advertises "F. M. Pointer The Old Reliable House Mover." A giant fish swims across the facade. A sign lists the day's river-fish specials: catfish, trout, perch, drum, buffalo, eel. The owner's motto is spelled out in large, can't-miss letters: "Honest Weights, Square Dealings." Great sign.

Evans's preoccupation with signs "extended far beyond the graphic elements and significant texts they might provide," Judith Keller writes in the book's introduction. "He admired signs as objects, collected them (whether from street corners or antique shops), and in the early 1970s, well before Post-modernism had arrived, he exhibited signs, sometimes next to his own photographic representations of them."

Signs serve as much more than commercial props. They provide a glimpse into everyday

Tampa.

Hollywood.

Norland.

life, into social and cultural issues and customs. They reflect the tenor of the neighborhood and the time. They may be simple and crude, but therein lies their charm. They're made by businessmen and women who don't have Madison Avenue budgets and must rely on the message, for the medium is often ordinary.

The signs in this chapter and the next are a random collection of pitches, pleas, persuasions, and in some cases, like the faded motel signs, reminders of Florida's glorious roadside past.

Let There Be Light

Is there anything more comforting and alluring along the road than a flickering, fiery neon sign? Whether advertising a restaurant, café, diner, ice cream stand, candy shop, miniature golf course, motel, or other roadside stop, a great neon sign draws you in with its illuminated magnificence and promise of food, gas, lodging, fun, and escape.

"Modern signage," says Len Davidson, "has largely gone in nonfigural directions. Much is bland and forgettable; a few back-lit plastic initials (with neon hidden inside) passes for a corporate logo. If you've never been turned on to neon, you probably haven't seen the good stuff."

He's seen the good stuff, having devoted a good part of his life to the pursuit of it. His book *Vintage Neon* is an absolute must to lovers of roadside Americana. Its 190 pages burst with marvelous examples of the neon sign maker's art: glowing hamburgers, flying pigs, swirly ice cream cones, syrup-topped pancakes, revolving windmills, smiling Buddhas, and tongue-flicking dragons. "Neon signs provide a sense of place," Davidson said. "Great signs are landmarks. Burning through evening's darkness, neon is a guidepost for finding one's way."

Blame his neon obsession on Florida. Davidson, who grew up in Philadelphia, started collecting and restoring vintage neon signs while teaching organizational behavior at the University of Florida. Whenever he had spare time, he would hop in his 1959 Impala and scour neon graveyards between Tampa and New Orleans for old signs. "I've been fascinated with the Florida roadside since the seventies," he said.

Perry.

In 1974, he met signmaker Jim Williams, owner of Williams Sign Company in Gainesville. Their shared fascination for neon and American pop culture led to their opening the Gamery in Gainesville, a tavern decorated with neon signs, superhero figures, pinball displays, and racing Lionel trains. The Gamery didn't last long—"We had no restaurant experience," Davidson conceded—but his passion for neon grew.

He eventually left academia to form Davidson Neon Design, a custom sign business. He fashioned his own signs from junked neon, electrical timers, and other discarded objects. By the time he moved back to Philly in 1979, his home was overrun with neon signs. But his search for vintage neon never lessened. "I'd spend mornings training executives, and then, Clark Kent–like, shed my business suit and go zooming through Metropolis on neon rescue missions," he recalled.

In 1985, he founded the Neon Museum of Philadelphia to showcase his collection. This is one museum you can't visit; Davidson operates it as a lending library, loaning his signs out free of charge to businesses that want to display them in their storefronts. Occasionally he organizes bus tours of the pieces.

Cocoa.

He still has several of the neon signs he collected while in Florida, but he has traded others. He traded a neon hamburger sign from a Gainesville restaurant for a Pep Boys neon sign, which he turned around and traded for a neon saw sign from a Philly hardware store.

How did neon begin? According to inventors.about.com, the French engineer and chemist Georges Claude was the first to apply an electrical discharge to a sealed tube of neon gas to create a lamp. The word *neon* comes from the Greek *neos*, meaning "the new gas." Claude displayed the first neon lamp to the public on December 11, 1910, in Paris. In 1923, he introduced neon gas signs to the United States by selling two Packard signs to a car dealership in Los Angeles for $24,000. "Neon lighting quickly became a popular fixture in outdoor advertising," says the website. "Visible even in daylight, people would stop and stare at the first neon signs, dubbed 'liquid fire.'"

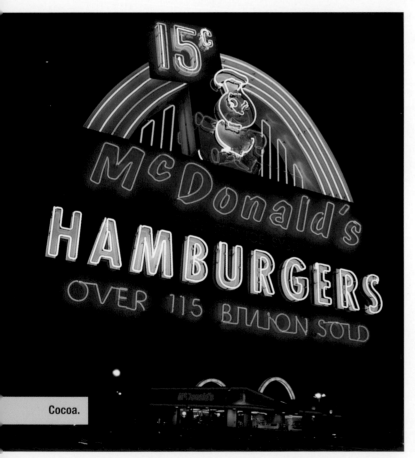

Cocoa.

The 1950s were the golden age of neon in America. "It was an intoxicating era of pouring wine bottles, Indian war bonnets and scampering monkeys—a boisterous neon epoch scarcely imaginable today," Davidson said. At the time, there were at least fifty neon "tubebenders" in Philadelphia alone; hundreds more worked in New York City. When Davidson moved back to Philly in 1979, only five or six tubebenders remained in the city.

The apogee of the neon sign was the animated piece: wine bottles that poured, waterfalls that cascaded, butchers that cut meat, horses that galloped, and birds that flapped their wings. Davidson calls the neon eagle at the Anheuser-Busch Brewery in St. Louis the most breathtaking animation he's ever seen. The eagle is twenty-six feet wide and thirty-two feet tall,

CARNIVAL HERE THIS WEEK!
FEAR FACTORY OPEN THURSDAY
CHECK IT OUT IF YOU DARE !

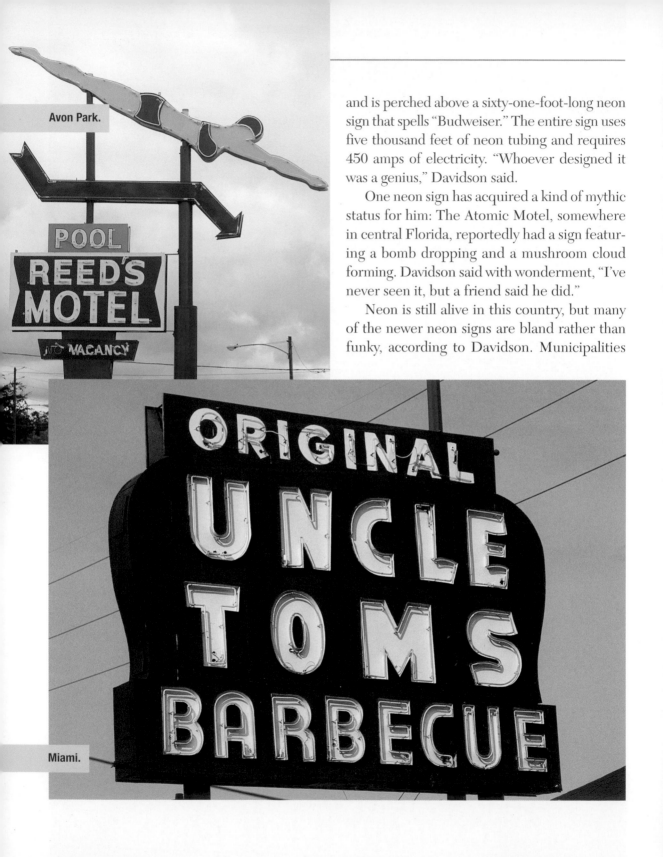

Avon Park.

POOL
REED'S
MOTEL
NO VACANCY

Miami.

ORIGINAL UNCLE TOMS BARBECUE

and is perched above a sixty-one-foot-long neon sign that spells "Budweiser." The entire sign uses five thousand feet of neon tubing and requires 450 amps of electricity. "Whoever designed it was a genius," Davidson said.

One neon sign has acquired a kind of mythic status for him: The Atomic Motel, somewhere in central Florida, reportedly had a sign featuring a bomb dropping and a mushroom cloud forming. Davidson said with wonderment, "I've never seen it, but a friend said he did."

Neon is still alive in this country, but many of the newer neon signs are bland rather than funky, according to Davidson. Municipalities

Orlando.

Daytona Beach Shores.

WELCOME
NEW GREENS
LIVE GATORS

Jacksonville.

Miami.

Holly Hill.

across the country have discouraged neon. Where it is present, it often occurs only inside plastic letters. "Architects—professionals who should know better," Davidson said, "commonly steer clients to plastic front signage. Neon's originality and exuberance are hard to swallow."

But the craft and art live on in vintage signs, as seen in these pages and in books like Davidson's. "Neon is folk art," he said. "Neon signs are campy in a good sense, cartoony in a good sense. It's all about the creative spirit in American culture."

The World's Largest Gators
and Other Giants along the Road

World's Second Largest Gator at Gator Motel, 4576 West Irlo Bronson Memorial Highway (Route192), Kissimmee.

Swampy at Jungle Adventures, 26205 East Highway 50, Christmas.

So you're a big, bad gator, the biggest, baddest gator of them all, 126 feet long, with beady eyes, fearsome-looking teeth, and a Matterhorn of a snout. Anchored along the side of Highway 192 in Kissimmee, you spend years terrorizing little tykes on the way to Disney World, a land cruiser dangling from your monstrous mouth and a look on your face that says, "If you get any closer I will eat you and your little sister for breakfast."

Then one day a bigger gator thunders into Florida, a bad boy nearly twice as big as you, and they call him Swampy, and he is now king of the roadside reptilian kingdom. What's a poor gator to do?

In the world of roadside giants, being number two and saying you'll try harder is not really an option. The World's Second Largest Alligator, stationed in front of the Gator Motel, remains a formidable sight. But in recent years, Swampy, big enough to hold the gift shop, ticket counter, and offices of Jungle Adventures in Christmas, has been getting most of

Two giants on buildings along Highway 192, Kissimmee.

the headlines. He's appeared on book covers and in magazine spreads and is the darling of broadcast crews everywhere, including a local TV news van that once backed over his tail and crushed the last three or four feet. Swampy was not amused.

"Roadside giants were built to catch the attention of potential customers with an extraordinary visual trick," say Brian and Sarah Butko, authors of *Roadside Giants*.

Florida, where kitsch is king and subtlety never a virtue, probably does bigger better than any other state. They know how to supersize here. Take just one road—Highway 192 through Kissimmee, where one roadside wonder after another vies for your attention. A magnificent white-bearded Merlin, giant scepter in hand, peers down from atop a gift shop. A voluptuous blond-haired mermaid is splashed across the facade of another. There are castles, Vikings, medieval towers, giant golf balls, a jukebox-shaped restaurant, and the self-proclaimed World's Largest Gift Shop. Even the signs and billboards are bigger than normal, seemingly muscling each other out of the way in an attempt to get your attention on a road that is part children's playground, part Times Square.

Inverness.

Giant-size signs, statues, and figures would seem to be a fairly modern phenomenon, but unnaturally large objects—giant potatoes, loaves of bread, ears of corn—appeared on "tall tale" postcards in the early 1900s, Karal Ann Marling writes in her seminal book *The Colossus of Roads*.

It was only a matter of time before larger-than-life signs, statues, and figures jumped from postcards and magazine ads to the American roadside, which was in need of life and color, not to mention order. Long-distance driving in the early 1920s, Marling notes, "was a nightmare of mixed turns, frantic hunts for landmarks and quarrels over whether the signpost at the last crossroads, bristling with hand-lettered

Treasure Island.

directional arrows, had or had not been rotated by pranksters."

The Federal Highway Act of 1921 brought order to the highway sign chaos. As highways improved and America hit the road, businesses tried ever more clever ways to get motorists' attention. In 1926, Allan Odell started putting up his Burma Shave signs in Minnesota. Wall Drugs told you how many miles remained to the famed drugstore in South Dakota. Billboards grew larger and larger, and with the help of Thomas Edison they were lit up at night.

By the 1920s, giant man-made oranges and lemons, functioning as juice stands, were sprouting in California. The Mother Goose Pantry Restaurant, a giant shoe with striped awnings, was operating in Pasadena. There were also an enormous spotted pig in Harlingen, Texas; a massive Sphinx outside Sphinx Realty in Los Angeles; and towering wigwam and tepee motels throughout the West.

Wayside giants, Marling argues, sold not only a specific product, but the American dream. "Colossi are advertisements that point to commodities for sale—resorts, or roadside curiosities, or, in the case of a big Paul Bunyan, an opportunity to escape from the gritty tedium of the highway into an amusing, diverting storybook legend."

The incomparable John Margolies says in *Fun along the Road* that small towns across America used oversize objects to put themselves on the tourist map and helped create a recognizable identity.

Thousands of giants towered and glowered over the American landscape in the 1940s and 1950s. Another wave marched across the land in the 1960s and early 1970s, when a California company, International Fiberglass, started building figures for restaurants, hotels, gas stations, miniature golf courses, and other businesses (see roadsideamerica.com/muffler).

The roadside giant, Marling observes, "is always a place in itself, where the everyday rules of reality are suspended and an idyllic dream commences. Grotesque scale demands a pause—for edification, for commerce, or for the fantastic fun of it."

Which brings us back to the World's Second Largest Gator, in Kissimmee. The unnamed monster will forever take a backseat to Swampy, but it still deserves admiration and respect. So what if there's a gator nearly twice its size an hour away? It is still a fearsome-looking beast, and it's bigger than every other gator on earth. Except one.

"For many years," reports roadsideamerica.com, "Kissimmee's giant gator reigned as the World's Largest. Its 126 feet of reptilian eye candy yanked family vanloads out of the tourist trap that flowed along Hwy. 192 into Disney." But in 1992, Swampy, all two hundred feet, one inch of him, sprang into existence. His teeth form the entrance to Jungle Adventures, on Highway 50 in the town of Christmas, between Orlando and Titusville. Inside is a twenty-acre park and wildlife sanctuary (see jungleadventures.com). There are gator feedings, jungle cruises, and a Native American village; the park is home to alligators, crocodiles, panthers, monkeys, snakes, and other animals.

Jungle Adventures started as Gator Jungle in 1989. When Swampy was built, Gatorland Zoo took Gator Jungle to court, alleging that the gaping doorway entrance to Swampy violated Gatorland Zoo's trademark and "would lure tourists to the wrong alligator farm," according to Vaughn L. Glasgow in *A Social History of the American Alligator*. The judge ruled that Swampy's giant jaws could be confused with those at Gatorland Zoo and said the doorway must be removed. Minor alterations were made, but the beast remained.

My favorite Florida roadside giant is not a gator, but a dinosaur: the graceful Sinclair Dino at Harold's Auto Center in Spring Hill. At the

Apalachicola.

Islamorada.

1964 New York World's Fair, the oil and gas company, whose corporate symbol was the brontosaurus, built an exhibit called Dinoland. "The exhibit featured nine full-size replicas of dinosaurs and inspired Sinclair's promotional department to build a dinosaur of its own," says J. J. C. Andrews in *The Well-Built Elephant and Other Roadside Attractions*.

Dino was built of steel ribbing, metal lath, and cement, at a cost of $25,000. He is one hundred feet long, thirty-four feet high, and thirty feet wide. Three garage bays fit comfortably inside his shell. When he was younger, Dino's eyes lit up. The eyes no longer shine, but the white

Sinclair Dino at Harold's Auto Center, Route 19, Spring Hill.

dinosaur remains a remarkable roadside attraction. Dana Hurst, the current owner, doesn't mind if you pull in and take a picture; he's used to it by now.

In a day of sterile strip malls, bland big-box stores, and humorless, hollow advertising, we could use more of the fun, colorful roadside giants. I'm sure Dino and Swampy—and the World's Second Largest Gator—would agree.

Wherefore Art Thou, Romeo?
West of Ocala, That's Where

Does any state have as many colorful-sounding towns and place names as Florida? From Mossy Head, Mayo, and Lulu in the north, to Frostproof, Balm, and Croom-A-Coochee in the middle, to Okeelanta, Opa-locka, and Okeechobee farther south, the Florida map is full of wit and whimsy. There's plenty to chew on, with towns like Two Egg, Mango, and Tangerine. Bagdad can be found here, and so can Switzerland, Havana, and Sumatra. The Sunshine State is home to "America's Sweetest Town" as well as a town proud of its "six old grouches." The Heart of the South is here, too.

I ran across nothing but nice people in my wanderings through Florida; one town in particular tries to live up to the name. **Niceville** is situated along the shores of Lake Choctawhatchee, just north of Fort Walton Beach and Destin.

For a while, though, some residents were unhappy about living in Niceville. The area was originally populated by Native Americans; by

the early 1800s, white settlers established a fishing village, named Boggy after Boggy Bayou, a local bay. A sawmill and general store were built, and in 1893, the U.S. Post Office officially recognized the city name of Boggy. But locals didn't think that was too flattering, so they changed it to Niceville. Some objected to that name, and it was changed to Valparaiso. But a town called New Valparaiso was forming a mile away, so in 1925, the town's name was changed back to Niceville, which it remains. Nice of them to end the confusion.

The biggest event on Niceville's social calendar is the annual Boggy Bayou Festival. Last year's festival featured the Charlie Daniels Band and Terri Clark.

"Whether you're in town for a day, month or the rest of your life, you won't be disappointed with Niceville!" says the town's official website, cityofniceville.org.

Ponce de Leon, just off I-10 in northwest Florida, is named after the Spanish explorer who searched for the Fountain of Youth. The Ponce De Leon Springs, in town, produces millions of gallons of crystal-clear water and is the centerpiece of a 443-acre state park, according to the town's website, poncedeleonfl.com. The town brags that it doesn't have a red light and offers "slower-paced living with plenty of elbow room." What is billed as the "Biggest All-Night Gospel Sing in the World" is held in Bonifay, fifteen miles away. Florida's oldest library is in DeFuniak Springs, ten miles away. Lake DeFuniak is said to be one of only two perfectly round natural lakes in the world.

Clewiston, "America's Sweetest Town," is located on the southwest shore of Lake Okeechobee—"a friendly little town of 6,500 people way out in the middle of nowhere," advertises the town's website. What qualifies as "the middle of nowhere" in Florida, anyway; the town is sixty miles east of Fort Myers and 60 miles west of Palm Beach.

The first permanent settlement was established in 1920. Within several years, the rich muck lands in the area attracted midwesterners eager to grow sugar cane. Extensive sugar cane plantations followed. The town became known as "America's Sweetest Town" thanks to the presence of the U.S. Sugar Corporation. Citrus, though, has become a big crop over the years; Hendry County, in which Clewiston is located, has more citrus trees than any county in Florida.

One of my favorite town welcome signs can be found in **Sebastian**, just north of Vero Beach and home of Pelican Island, the first designated wildlife refuge in the United States. "Friendly People and Six Old Grouches," reads Sebastian's welcome sign. The population of old grouches must have exploded in recent years; I remember when the sign read, "One Old Grouch." The identity of the original grouch is not

known. A 1983 account on the town library website, sebastianlibrary
.com, sheds little light on the mystery:

> The city of Sebastian has authorized its city clerk to ask for bids for the
> erection of welcoming signs on U.S. 1 at both the north and south city
> limits. A.T. Jordan, Sebastian's city clerk, is proposing this wording for
> the signs: "Welcome to Sebastian—687 Friendly People and One Old
> Grouch." If hard pressed by any Sebastian citizen to say just who that old
> grouch may be, Jordan is prepared to refer them to his own wife and
> daughters. "They have to put up with me year in and year out," Jordan is
> frank to admit.

The people in one heartland community love to paint their town red —
and a bunch of other colors. The welcome sign for **Lake Placid** describes
it as the "Caladium Capital of the World," a reference to the tropical orna-
mental plant known for its colorful leaves. Caladiums were first grown in
the Lake Placid area in the early 1940s; twelve hundred acres are now
owned and managed by fourteen families. Drive through town in the sum-

mer, when the leaves burst into a rainbow of colors. The Caladium Festival, held in August, includes bus tours to the caladium fields, plus food, entertainment, arts and crafts booths, and a classic car show.

Walk through town, and you'll see Lake Placid's other claim to fame. Nearly forty murals cover the sides of buildings and even a few trash containers. A mural of the caladium fields, painted by Tom Freeman, adorns Lockhart Service Center on Interlake Boulevard.

My favorite mural, though, is the one titled *Tropical Bank Robbery*, at the corner of Main Street and Interlake Boulevard. Painted by Richard Currier, it shows the first bank robbery in Lake Placid, in 1931. Ten-year-old Grady Parrish was waiting for a haircut when someone pointed out two men, one in a red wig, the other in a black one, walking past the shop. The inquisitive Grady followed the men, who walked into the bank and announced it was a stickup. Grady ran to get his dad, who told him to get the marshal, who shot one of the robbers. Both were eventually apprehended. The marshal was given a $100 reward by the bank; Grady received $10. The mural can be found at the location of the Tropical State Bank, which burned down in 1991. For more information on Lake Placid and its murals, visit lpfla.com.

Havana, several miles north of Tallahassee, is "smokin' again," according to the website funandsun.com. "North Florida's Arts and Antiques Capital" is a picturesque town of shops and cafés. Twenty years ago, Havana, once home to a thriving tobacco industry, was pretty much a ghost town. In 1983, Tallahassee antique shop owners Keith Henderson and Lee Hotchkiss were interested in buying part of an old brick

warehouse in Havana; they ended up buying the entire block. They sold and leased the space, more dealers moved in, and Havana was back on the map again.

Today the town has thirty-plus shops, offering art, antiques, books, collectibles, jewelry, clothing, and gifts. There are twelve shops alone inside the Main Street Market, including the Market Café. Don't miss the annual Havana MusicFest, in April.

Harlem, just off Highway 27 in Hendry County, is an otherwise quiet town that comes to life during its annual Brown Sugar Festival. Held the first weekend in May, this is a celebration of the local sugar cane industry. Harlem began as a shanty-town of migrant workers and now has three thousand residents. The Brown Sugar Festival is "a black heritage and cultural festival with lots of soul food, out-of-this-world barbecue and exhibits," according to visithendrycounty.com.

Beverly Hills, southwest of Ocala, seems a peaceful enough community. "Where every day is just one more," the welcome sign announces rather existentially. The local Boy Scout troop, no. 452, sounds as if it wants to raise some hell. "We're on Fire!" proclaims the troop's website. A bit lower-keyed, presumably, is the Cracker Quilters Citrus County guild based in town.

Many people think *Boca Raton* means "rat's mouth," but few realize the town's name had nothing to do with a rodent problem. According to the official city website, ci.boca-raton.fl.us, "the Spanish word *boca* (or mouth), often described an inlet, while *raton* (literally mouse) was used as a term for a cowardly thief." Thieves Inlet, or *Boca Ratones*, was used on maps for an inlet in Biscayne Bay in the 1700s, but in the next century was erroneously used for Lake Boca Raton.

Mayo, northwest of Gainesville, is named after James Mayo, a colonel in the Confederate Army. He gave a speech one Fourth of July; settlers were so impressed they named the town after him. The local newspaper is called the *Mayo Free Press*.

Sopchoppy, in Wakulla County, derives its name from Lockchoppe, the name of a river. *Lokchapi* is Muskogee for red oak. **Yeehaw** is a corruption of the Muskogee *yaha*, which means wolf. Yeehaw Junction, "the crossroads of Florida," is home to the historic Desert Inn, website desertinnrestaurant.com.

On December 25, 1837, a contingent of two thousand U.S. Army soldiers and Alabama Volunteers arrived at a spot in central Florida and named it, appropriately enough, **Fort Christmas**. The town, about twenty miles east of Orlando, is home of Fort Christmas Historical Park and the World's Largest Gator. Swampy's his name, and you'll find him in an earlier chapter.

For the lowdown on thousands of forgotten towns around the country, check out the terrific website ghosttowns.com. It provides capsules and bygone photos of about 150 Florida towns, from Acron and Andytown to Rattlesnake, Tasmania, and **Welcome**. This last one, in Hillsborough County, was created by the Florida Peninsular Railroad at the turn of the twentieth century. Rivers Grocery served as a post office from 1907 to 1911 and again from 1914 to 1916. The grocery stayed open until 1980, when Mrs. Rivers died. Wonder if the town ever had a "Welcome to Welcome" sign.

Mike Woodfin hates to break the news to you. "There never was a fort" at **Fort Lonesome**, he says on ghosttowns.com. After the town suffered a fruit fly outbreak in 1929, one health inspector put up a sign reading "Fort Lonesome." In the 1930s, it became a boom town with the opening of a sawmill. Fort Lonesome "was a place on a Saturday night your Momma told you stay away from," Woodfin relates. Today little is left of Fort Lonesome except a few homes and a convenience store.

Nearby are **Balm** and **Picnic**. A general store in Balm offers these services: "Information Groceries

Telephone Notary Restroom Copies." The town, according to ghosttowns.com, was originally known as Doris; it became Balm in June 1902. The Sweat family, descendants of some of the earliest settlers, still live in Balm.

Picnic was never a town. According to Mike and Aaron Woodfin, "The residents figure the name came from the fact that two wooden bridges crossed the creek there and it was the community place for a picnic in the 1900s."

On any list of memorable Florida place names, **Kismet** would have to rank near the top. It was founded, according to Woodfin, by the Kismet Land and Improvement Company. It had a post office, sawmill, tavern, and the splendid Grand View Motel, which was later moved to Eustis. Kismet does not appear on the official state map; the area is part of the Ocala National Forest.

Walter Gillen was so enamored of his girlfriend he named a town, **Lulu**, after her. Gillen, according to ghosttowns.com, persuaded the Georgia Southern Florida Railroad to build a station in this section of Columbia County. Lulu grew to include two cotton gins, a one-room school, three churches, two barbershops, and a handful of stores. "The citizens of Lulu had hoped that their community would become a thriving town but the boll weevil came and destroyed the cotton business," resident Kim Croft writes on the website. Today about three hundred people live in Lulu.

Romeo was settled as early as the 1850s, but even ghosttowns.com is not sure of the name's origin or whether there was a Juliet involved.

If there's one Florida town name no one can agree on, it's **Two Egg**, not far from where Florida, Alabama, and Georgia meet. The riotously funny website http://members.aol.com/bettymaes/twoegg.html lists a dozen different stories behind the town's name, submitted by people who all swear theirs is the correct version.

It was named by salesmen who observed store customers bartering for two eggs' worth of tobacco, sugar, and other supplies; it was named because local kids would bring two eggs to trade for candy; it was named by a traveling preacher because the local family putting him up for the night would be paid two eggs; it was named because the first sale at the store was two eggs; and . . . well, you get the idea.

"There are more theories about the town than there are residents," someone wisely observes on the website. "It's best not to claim that you know the most accurate version."

You Have Permission to Be Yourself

Just off North Miami Avenue in Miami, within earshot of a mammoth retail-commercial project under construction, stands an otherwise drab white house that has something to say.

"Never Put Out Your Blaze for the Comfort of Others," reads one of the slogans painted in big, black letters on the house. "I Dream of a World United Filled with People of Clear Perspective" sneaks across the side wall. Various words are painted on the front of the house: "Share. Hope. Trust. Clarity. Faith. Vision. Dream. Reason. Reality. Love. Peace."

Somehow, in a city as slick and stylish as Miami, the plain, block-lettered messages on N.W. 31st Street manage to get your attention. Call it guerrilla art or drive-by art—or just Michael Tronn's way of making you think.

"A general theme of my work is breaking down barriers to social awareness," says the thirty-five-year-old artist. "Why we think what we think, and if it's appropriate to think what we think."

The house is called the Urban Art Farm, a 1924 structure Tronn bought three years ago. No one lives there; Tronn uses it as an art gallery. He has done several photo exhibits inside the Farm, but the sayings painted outside are what catch the eye of passers-by.

"I try to be very straightforward and easy to understand," he explains. "You don't want to make it too complicated."

But Tronn, an artist and photographer, lives a complicated life. Once a key figure in the New York City club scene, his face appearing on the cover of *New York* magazine as a founder of the so-called "club kid" movement, Tronn is active today in the Miami club scene. He has enlisted the likes of Madonna, Mark Anthony, and Junior Vasquez to appear at his Anthem parties ("Miami's most renowned event!") at the Mansion and Metropolis clubs. He serves on the board of directors of the Miami Gay and Lesbian Film Festival. He is forever shooting photographs of whatever strikes his fancy; for one exhibit, he took 15,000 photos, whittling it down to 115. He is working on a short film about the "glamorous superficiality" of the local club scene.

"Coasting," he says, "has never been my MO."

Born in New York, he attended an arts and science high school in the city. What did he want to be when he grew up? An astronaut? President of the United States?

Urban Art Farm, 50 N.W. 31st Street, Miami.

Michael Tronn's works at Urban Art Farm.

"I never wanted to be an astronaut!" he replies, laughing. "But I don't think I ever wanted to be an artist, either." Nonetheless, he started taking art lessons when he was three; his mom still has one of his pre-kindergarten-age paintings.

He eventually enrolled at Parsons School of Design in both New York City and Paris but says he found the experience very boring. He returned to New York when he was nineteen, worked as art director for an agency, then began flirting with the city club scene. "An incredible social dynamic was going on in New York; artists happened to congregate in the clubs," he recalls.

He started showing his art in 1986, when he did shows of his hand-painted clothing at noted clubs the Saint and the Tunnel. In 1987, he befriended renowned pop artist Keith Haring, working with him on the Statue of Liberty Project in New York City and the Brandywine Project in Philadelphia.

In 1989, Tronn did a solo show of sculpture, paintings, photos, and illustrations at the Red Zone. In 1992, he switched to what he calls pop pointillism—paint dots on canvas, done by hand, creating portraits of Madonna, Andy Warhol, Princess Diana, and others. Then he did an exhibit in Mexico using heavy, black free-form lines over gold canvases to depict humanity.

"I went down for what was supposed to be a week, and it was extended and extended and extended," he says, laughing. "I ended up being there six months."

On a vacation trip to Miami, Tronn met and started working for the owners of the club Liquid. One account described "the bubbling hot Liquid" as "the extreme of celebrity chic clubs." Its opening-night roster included Calvin Klein, David Geffen, and Gloria Estefan, and Madonna and Rosie O'Donnell, among others, were frequent guests.

"Liquid offers a constant stream of creative, cool events encompassed by celebrities," Tronn told Peggy Wallace of beveragenet.net. "We're always surprising people with what we do. We'll have drag performers, celebrity parties, fashion shows."

The club offered "living installations" on the dance floor, including whipped-cream-covered nude models and leather-chap-clad men astride rocking horses.

Later, Tronn helped transform Crobar, on West 28th Street in New York. A 2003 item in Michael Musto's celebrated "La Dolce Musto" column chronicled Tronn's latest creative project:

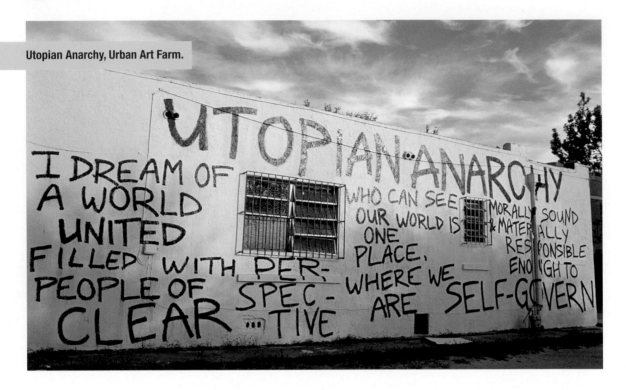

Utopian Anarchy, Urban Art Farm.

"We want it to be a scene, not just a money scene," club-kid-turned-idea-guy Michael Tronn said on a hard-hat tour last week. And so, at the entrance will be a DNA wall of monitors ("very conceptual, not cheesy," assured Tronn) and inside, there's a giant dance floor, an apartment-like side room, and another special area that's very "Barbarella meets ski lodge." And good news for waxed straight guys: There's no gay night per se, but there'll be metrosexual ones!

These days, Tronn is concentrating on his art and other creative projects. An exhibit he did at the Diaspora Vibe Gallery was the precursor of the Urban Art Farm. The exhibit, titled "33.1 InsiTions," was composed of thirty-three twelve-foot high unbleached muslins with black-painted slogans:

"When the Real You Surfaces You Will Shine with the Light of
    a Million Suns"
"We Only Hate Others When We Do Not Love Ourselves"
"Why Do They Lead Us with Tyranny and Fear and Why Do
    We Follow?"

"You Have Permission to Be Yourself"
"Have You Sold Your Dreams for the Pursuit of Possessions?"
"I Hear Your Soul Crying Even If You Don't"

A friend who works for the city of Miami told Tronn about the then-vacant house on N.W. 31st Street, saying, "This is *your* house." Tronn bought the building three years ago. "The intention of the Farm was always to nurture the art scene down there," Tronn says.

South of Arcadia.

Eastpoint.

Art murals in
Jacksonville.

He painted the words himself, taking about a week to complete the project. The people in the neighborhood at first were "perplexed, but they grew to love it and support it," he says. The only one to make a fuss about it was the city of Miami, which wanted me to paint it over. My attorney sent them a letter and that was that."

No one has defaced the words or the house, which the artist finds amazing. "It means they get it and they're accepting of it," he says.

The Urban Art Farm is one of about sixty galleries and alternative spaces that make up the Wynwood Art District, bordered by N.W. 6th Avenue to the west, North Miami Avenue to the east, N.W. 36th Street to the north, and N.W. 10th Street to the south.

Another exhibit at the Farm was titled "Vengeance #2: Fuck. Shame. Strip. Fear," which was composed of nude self-portraits of Tronn. "It was too outrageous for even *New Times* [a local alternative newspaper] to run a story on," he explains. "The exhibit did great; it just didn't get any press."

So how did he get the word out?

"Promotion," he says, smiling, "is not a problem with me."

Neither are finding time to create and stirring up commotion every once in a while.

"I'm an ambitious person," he says. "I enjoy creating. I'm always writing down an idea. I definitely do create a lot. It's a lot more fun than playing Parcheesi."

The Friendliest Man on Earth

Jimbo Luznar of Jimbo's, Duck Lake Road, Virginia Key.

It's cocktail hour at the bar that time forgot. Regulars slouch on battered plastic chairs, their cars and trucks parked at odd angles in the hard-packed sand driveway. Cats poke around in the rubbish. Three shrimp boats that look like they came under aerial bombardment are tied up at the dock. A girl in her mid-twenties climbs up into the bleachers overlooking the bocce court, sits down, and promptly falls asleep.

Want a beer? Walk into the decrepit tin-roofed shack, fish a Bud or Corona from the cooler, and pay the man sitting on the chair outside.

"I'd rather talk than drink, I'll tell you that," announces a raspy-voiced seventy-eight-year-old man in a green polo shirt and baseball cap.

It's 9:15 A.M. At Jimbo's, pretty much any hour is cocktail hour.

"This place gives me a chance to see all my good friends in Miami," says Jimbo Luznar, in the green shirt. "I probably have more friends in Miami than the mayor."

When you run the ultimate dive bar and you are, as his website proclaims, "the friendliest man on earth," your friends will be legion. Some of them may even be sober. Welcome to Jimbo's, Virginia Key, Miami. You can see the city skyline from Jimbo's dock, but Miami might as well be the moon.

There's no bar to speak of; just grab a beer and find a chair or plop on the dock. There are no happy-hour specials; Buds are $2, and Heineken, Becks, and Corona $3, whether you're drinking at 9 A.M. or 9 P.M. There is no food or music, except at the occasional party; no restrooms—use the Porta-Potties; and certainly no wet T-shirt contests, although Jimbo always seems to find himself in a happy embrace with one of the bikini-clad young women who frequent the place.

Jimbo's is probably the most-photographed dive bar in America; it seems as if there's always a magazine spread or movie being shot here. A dozen episodes of *Miami Vice*, along with several of *Flipper*, were filmed here. So was *True Lies*, with Arnold Schwarzenegger and Jamie Lee

Jimbo's.

Curtis. As Jimbo talks to me, a Latino model in a lime green thong poses seductively on the hood of a yellow school bus, part of the abandoned-vehicle graveyard at Jimbo's.

The shack is a collection of lashed-together beams; think Robinson Crusoe on a perpetual happy hour. Smoke pours from a rusty fifty-five-gallon drum; goodness knows what's burning in there. A shark jaw adorns a wall. Those expecting such basics as bartenders, tables, and air-conditioning should probably go elsewhere.

"This beautiful model was sitting on my lap right here," Jimbo says of one photo shoot. "It was Miss Alabama." He laughs heartily. "Boy, I've had a lot of fun."

First-timers blend easily with regulars, German backpackers with Miami attorneys. Everyone seems to walk around a bit bleary-eyed, and you would, too, if you started drinking around 9 A.M.

The Friendliest Man on Earth? You'll get no argument from me. I walked up to him and said, "I'm looking for the friendliest man in Florida." He grinned from ear to ear, shook my hand, and launched immediately into his life story. He talked for an hour, got up to refill his drink, then talked for another hour, pausing only to have his picture taken with a young blond in a plunging bikini top. He sat down, picking up the life story where he had left off. Never once did he ask me why I was writing everything down so furiously, although I did tell him.

Jimbo might be the Friendliest Man in the Universe. He says he's seventy-eight but feels like forty. "There are days when it's cold and it takes a while to get the knees going, but once I get going, I can do anything."

How he ended up on Virginia Key, right across the street from a city sewage plant (used to stink, doesn't anymore), is worth a book on its own. Born in western Maryland, he worked on the railroad when he was sixteen. "I learned so much as a machine apprentice," he says, "that when I got to school to train for a seaman, I knew more than the instructors. I knew everything."

His parents were from Yugoslavia; his father worked for Dizzy Dean's grandfather at a sawmill in Arkansas. He served in the merchant marine during World War II, returned to Maryland, and opened a pool hall. He met his future wife.

"On July 13 it will be fifty-seven years with the same woman," he says. "My love for that woman was so strong." They have five children; Jimbo is one of fourteen brothers and sisters.

His father moved the family to Samsula, between Deland and New Smyrna Beach; Jimbo worked on a shrimp boat out of New Smyrna. He moved to Miami in the early 1950s. He kept his shrimp boat tied up near Biscayne Boulevard. The city had plans for the area, so Jimbo and other fishermen had to clear out. The city offered Jimbo a piece of land to rent on Virginia Key.

"They forced me to come down here fifty years ago when all that was down here was that crap plant and a whole bunch of mosquitoes," he begins, a big, fat stogie in his hand. "They didn't do me no favor putting me here."

If he sounds bitter, it's for good reason. In recent years, the city and developers have cast covetous eyes on Virginia Key; about eight years ago, a proposal for high-end condos was scuttled after opposition from locals.

"We got petitions from people in Miami, from all over the world," Jimbo says. "The city is waiting for a hurricane to come take me out of here. If I live another twenty years, the people who have been trying to get me out will be gone."

Mike and Loren Shanley love Jimbo's.

Miami.

Marathon.

Sebring.

It may be a dive bar, but it's Miami's dive bar; local pols have been known to pull up a chair.

"This is old Florida; this is the way it was before everything changed," says Jimbo's regular Mike Shanley, owner of BoatNation USA, which sells used boats. "I think a lot of people come here reaching for that simplicity."

Jimbo's is not just for grizzled old-timers. Shanley brings his daughter Loren, and there are often kids scampering out on the dock. The yard is home to a collection of scruffy but much-loved cats and dogs; a rooster crows nearby.

One sign tells clientele not to drink within fifty feet of the premises, a warning clearly not taken seriously. Jimbo still occasionally goes out on his shrimp boat; a sign spells out his rules of the sea:

"**Yes** The Shrimp Are Small
No I Don't Know Why
Yes They Are All the Same
No I Can't Just Pick All Big Ones
Yes I Know You're a Good Customer
No You Can't Pick Them Yourself
Yes There Is Still 12 in a Dozen
No We Don't Have Live Mullet
Yes I Lose Count if I Answer Questions
No I Don't Grow Them, Just Catch and Sell
Yes They Are Always Small in Summer
Any Further Questions, Ask the Shrimp"

The bar's roof came from an elementary school in Miami. "They took it off, threw it in the garbage," Jimbo says. "It's a composite of coconut husk and all that stuff. The tin flies off, you pick it up, put it back on."

Parked out front are two battered pickups and a Mercedes. Good luck finding a parking spot at Jimbo's annual birthday party, held the Sunday closest to his actual birthday, April 6. About twenty-five hundred people showed up at the last one. There were thirty-six kegs of beer, fifteen hundred burgers, one thousand hotdogs. There is music, mirth, and mild mayhem.

"It's just like what that sign over there says—miles away from ordinary," Jimbo tells me as he surveys his kingdom. "It's different than anywhere else in the world."

Breakfast for him this morning seems to consist of his vodka and orange juice and a bag of chicharrones, or pork rinds, which a friend brings from a shop in Miami.

Yeehaw Junction.

Miami.

Sebring.

"You know who had their picture taken right there?" he asks, pointing to the shack doorway. "Mariah Carey. Jack Nicholson was here; he died on my dock." In the movie *Blood and Wine*, anyway.

The first movie filmed here was the less-than-classic *Island Claws*, about a humongous killer crab. The row of colorful faux-Bahamian shacks on the property were built for the movie.

"They had this forty-foot-long plastic crab, came out of the water," Jimbo recalls. "They put it on a tractor. Then they let loose a thousand little crabs—they were supposed to be the babies of the big crab."

He lives in North Miami Beach, up around 183rd Street. He calls his yard a "nature paradise," with eight big oaks. All his neighbors hire guys to cut their lawns; not Jimbo. "It keeps me fit." He's had two knees replaced. Shortly after one operation, he could barely walk, but his yard needed cutting. So he did it using a walker.

The bocce court is a fixture at Jimbo's. Challenge anyone to a game or just sit in the bleachers and watch. How did someone of Yugoslavian heritage get hooked on bocce? When he was a kid in Maryland, Jimbo's family lived near a Catholic church.

"The elderly Italian men would go to early Mass, go home, get a bottle of homemade wine, and play bocce at a court by the baseball field," Jimbo recalls. "They wouldn't leave until they finished all the wine. They let us kids play. Today they play this game all over the goddamn world. Argentina. Brazil. I was in France, they were playing bocce."

He still plays, and he's still pretty damn good.

Jimbo's, according to southbeachvibes.com, is "hands down the most difficult to find and even more difficult to describe watering hole in Miami. . . . The term bar doesn't begin to do this place justice."

Its owner is not easy to pin down, either.

"I don't want no fame," he says, reflective. "I just want to be me, I just want to live like me."

He cradles his bag of chicharrones, then suddenly rises from his chair. "I've got to leave," he says. "I could tell you so many stories about this place. You're going to fill up that one notebook and you're going to have to get another."

On the Road Again

There are 119,784 miles of road in Florida, according to the state Department of Transportation. I didn't drive all 119,784 miles while researching this book; it only seems as though I did.

As Floridians well know, some highways in the Sunshine State are more interesting than others. Is any road more wonderful, and less interesting, than the Florida Turnpike? Gets you where you want to go, but stay awake; there's absolutely nothing to see. I called U.S. 1 "America's best damn highway" in an earlier book, *The Great American Road Trip: US 1, Maine to Florida,* and I still believe it. It'll always have a special place in my heart—and gas tank.

But what is Florida's best, most interesting, most colorful road? That's a tough one. Four highways you can quickly disqualify: I-95, I-4, I-75, and the turnpike. Fine highways all, but interstates and toll roads by definition cannot be interesting.

Much of the fun researching this book came in wandering—a good part of it randomly and aimlessly— around the state. Many of the more colorful pictures in the book came from driving down major thoroughfares in the big cities: Miami, Tampa–St. Pete, Orlando, Jacksonville, and others. Roads like Highway 7/441 through Miami and Fort Lauderdale, Highway 192 in Kissimmee, Highway 27 from Miami to Tallahassee, A1A down the coast.

And Highway 98. It hasn't appeared on any list of most memorable Florida highways, as far as I know. It is not the fastest or most photogenic route. It doesn't even run in anything remotely resembling a straight line. It twists and turns from West Palm Beach to Pensacola and the Alabama state line, a staggering 647 miles in all. No, you can't drive it in a day. No, there aren't a lot of things to do along it. There are no world-class museums and few fancy restaurants; you're more apt to run across places like Deep South Family BBQ, outside Brooksville, or Hog Wild Bar-B-Cue, near Carabelle.

But the highway makes for plenty of pure, unadulterated, wind-in-your-hair-type driving (I admit I don't know what *that* feels like). Highway 98 needs an agent; it gets no publicity, no love. No one will ever write a book about it or dedicate a song to it. It's just not that sexy.

But it's one of the more colorful, quirky, loopy, meandering, and memorable highways in Florida—and the country. It's not a chamber of commerce kind of highway; you won't find anything about it on the Internet. But it takes you to parts of Florida you didn't know existed, to places so unlike Florida—or at least the common perception of Florida—that you may often wonder if you're in another state.

I want to take you on a journey from one end of 98 to the other, to prove that the most innocent-looking roads—not just in Florida, but anywhere—can be joys to drive, if you keep your eyes open. The highway uncoils at U.S. 1 in West Palm Beach and slithers its way up and across the state, circling Lake Okeechobee, passing through Sebring,

Mexico Beach.

Sebring.

Lakeland, and Dade City before darting along the Gulf Coast toward
Apalachicola, Panama City, Fort Walton Beach, and Pensacola.

Ignore its unremarkable beginning, at a West Palm intersection
marked by BP and Sunoco gas stations, Jon Smith Subs, and Brazilian
Jiu-Jitsu, whatever that is. Leave the beach and the boredom behind,
and head west and north. One of the first towns you'll hit is Sand Cut,
the "Speck Capital of the World." It's a tiny speck of a town, but that's
not how it got its nickname. Speck are black crappie or speckled perch,
found throughout Florida and especially in Lake Okeechobee, next to
which Sand Cut can be found.

There's a long stretch of lonesome from here to Sebring; it's part of
98's appeal. High-tension lines march across the flat landscape; oncoming trucks shimmer in the haze. A U.S. Sugar Corporation company village is in Bryant. The sign in front of a roadside market announces,
"Rabbits. Coons. Produce."

Several miles beyond Sand Cut comes the first glimpse of the awesome Okeechobee. J&S Fish Camp, Big Bass RV Park, and Gail's Bait Pail announce that you're in the middle of some of the best fishing anywhere. "If you want to catch big bass," says the website maintained by the Lake Okeechobee Guide Association, "the Big O is the place to go."

Cracker Trail Gun and Pawn can be found on 98 in Okeechobee, right next to the Wal-Mart. Calling a Floridian a "cracker" is not an insult; many longtime residents wear the badge proudly. The Florida Cracker Trail runs from Fort Pierce to Bradenton, taking in parts of Highways 98, 64, and 66. And there's an authentic nineteenth-century Cracker homestead at the Forest Capital Museum State Park on Highway 19/98 in Perry, southeast of Tallahassee.

"All arteries lead to Florida Hospital," announces a cheery billboard outside Sebring. A wrecked car with a missile jutting from its hood sits by the side of the highway, just south of the Sebring city limits. "Got Saddam," reads the spray-painted message, the work of a collision repair shop.

Homosassa Springs.

Near Avon Park is the Air Force's Avon Park Gunnery and Bombing Range, a "popular spot for camping and hunting," according to one description. Really. A sizable chunk of the 106,000-acre range is open for public access to hiking, hunting, fishing, camping, and other activities.

Frostproof, on 98, is the hub of the Florida citrus industry. How did it get its cool name? When the local post office rejected the proposed name Keystone City because it might be confused with Keystone Heights, locals submitted the name Lakemont. Joe Carson, a real estate broker, suggested Frostproof because he hoped to make his fortune buying and selling land for orange groves. The mayor listened as Carson made his case but wrote Lakemont on a form to be signed by the postmaster in Fort Meade. Carson offered to deliver the form. When it was returned, approved, the name Frostproof was written on it. Carson had pulled a fast one, crossing out Lakemont and substituting Frostproof.

Initially, the town didn't live up to its name. Frostproof suffered its first recorded frost on December 29, 1894; a second came the following February. Embarrassed residents petitioned successfully to have the name changed back to Lakemont, but the powerful Carson family had it changed back for good in 1906.

Crystal River.

Funky Fiddler in Panacea.

Kellie Boxberger of Funky Fiddler.

Highway 98 takes you through Lakeland. The town, with its parks, lakes, and Spanish-mission buildings, boasts one of the postcard-prettiest downtowns in Florida. "Jump First, Fear Later," announces a church sign. Florida Southern College features the world's largest collection of Frank Lloyd Wright–designed buildings.

Forty miles north is Dade City, home of the Men from Mars, presented in an earlier chapter, and the Pioneer Florida Museum. Located on a twenty-acre wooded hillside, the museum includes ten historic buildings, including an 1870s church, a 1920s general store, and a 1930s school. Neat place.

M. C. Chef ("Your soul food connection") and the Coney Island Drive-In are on 98 in

Carabelle.

Brooksville. Dig the mermaids, dolphins, sharks, miniature lighthouses, and other roadside kitsch at the rambling gift shop on 98 just south of Homosassa Springs. The highway begins its swing up the Gulf Coast, winding through Gulf Hammock, Otter Creek, and Chiefland. It's Peanutville through here; roadside stands like Maria's Dixie Nut House and Jake's Fried P-Nuts offer salty satisfaction.

A sign in Cross City, west of Gainesville, offers this inspirational message: "God Bless America. Be Safe. Be Brave. All-You-Can-Eat Buffet."

Route 98 is the best way to see and experience Florida's seven-hundred-mile-long Nature Coast. It's the other Florida, the one of woods, wildlife, and small towns. "Looking for trained seals and chickens that play pianos? You'll have to look elsewhere."

Tiny Panacea bills itself as the blue crab capital of the world; the Blue Crab Festival, in early May, is held in Wooley Park, overlooking scenic Dickerson Bay. Looking for colorful, one-of-a-kind souvenirs and craft items? Stop in the Funky Fiddler, owned by Kellie Boxberger. You'll find her on the porch, handpainting buckets or making jewelry or signs. I have a couple of her buckets, plus a "Shhh . . . Naked Mermaids Sleeping" sign.

While you're in the area, you might as well do some worm gruntin'. Sopchoppy, several miles west of Panacea on Route 319, is home to the annual Worm Gruntin' Festival. Worm gruntin' is a method of harvesting worms by hammering a wood stake in the ground and rubbing it with a filelike piece of metal. The vibrations send the worms to the surface. The Worm Gruntin' Festival, held in April, kicks off with the Worm Grunters' 5K Run. The Wakulla County Horseshoe Championship is held during the one-day festival, and so are the Worm Gruntin' Ball and the crowning of the Worm Monarch. Those folks in Sopchoppy know how to have fun.

Highway 98 winds gracefully along the Gulf of Mexico, St. George Sound, and Apalachicola Bay; this is known as Florida's Forgotten Coast.

Panama City Beach.

Ho-Hum RV Park is located just south of Carabelle. Ho-Hum nothing; this is pretty close to paradise. If I ever retire to Florida, it'll be along this stretch of highway. I've got a couple spots already picked out.

Visit the nation's smallest police station, the phone-booth-size substation in Carabelle. A sign outside Hog Wild Bar-B-Cue says the ribs are "Worth Driving 100 Miles For." Apalachicola is a historic town, and 98 takes you right through it. Looking for good, fresh seafood? Stop at Boss Oyster, right on the water. The

Destin.

DANGER:
HIGH VOLTAGE
KEEP OUT!

Apalachicola Seafood Grill serves "the world's largest fried fish sandwich." More than 90 percent of Florida's oysters are harvested in Franklin County, of which Apalachicola is part.

West of Port Joe, you enter the central time zone. As the *Florida Almanac* points out, Jacksonville is directly south of Cleveland and Pensacola directly south of Chicago, so Florida is more a midwestern than an eastern state. Yet all but a portion of the Panhandle is in the eastern time zone.

Another half hour west, and you're in the party zone. During spring break, Panama City and Panama City Beach become Boys and Girls Gone Wild, but it's delightful year-round. A must-stop is Thomas Donuts in Laguna Beach, right across from the water. Great donuts, greater view.

It's practically all commercial clutter and kitsch from here to Pensacola. The front of a psychedelic-painted Volkswagen bus juts from the face of Fudpuckers in Destin. A World World II vintage cargo plane seems to take flight at a miniature golf course, also in Destin. There's a sign for Watercolor on 98; it's a 499-acre coastal resort and residential community.

Highway 98 leaps Pensacola Bay and takes multiple twists and turns through the city; stay alert. Another Goofy Golf is on 98 (Navy Boulevard) in Pensacola. It's not as campy as its sister course in Panama City Beach, but it's well worth a visit.

Warrington, Myrtle Grove—we're getting close. And then, in a patch of woods just past the Crazy Horse Cafe, 98 ends suddenly and quietly. Just over the bridge is Alabama.

It's been nearly seven hundred miles, and several days, since we left West Palm Beach. We've come to the end of our journey—and this book. I hope it'll be the beginning, or continuation, of yours. If this book

Goofy Golf in Pensacola.

inspires you to take the road less traveled, then it has accomplished its mission. If it persuades you to check out places like Mango and Mayo, Corkscrew and Croom-A-Coochee, then I've done my job. There are plenty of roads like 98 in Florida; hop on one and give it a ride.

Thanks for picking up this book. May *your* road go on forever.

Highway Hangouts

Where would I have been without the memorable bars and restaurants in the year and a half I spent working on this book? Well, thirsty, for one thing, and hungry, for another.

These are a few of my favorite places.

Bars

Alabama Jack's, Card Sound
Boar's Nest, U.S. 1 North, Fort Lauderdale
Bonnie and Clyde's, Crescent City
Boot Hill Saloon, Daytona Beach
Herb's Limestone Grocery and Country Club, Limestone
Hog Heaven, Islamorada
Hog's Breath Saloon, Key West
Jimbo's, Virginia Key
Last Chance Saloon, Florida City
Last Resort, Port Orange
Mahuffer's/Sloppy John's, Indian Shores
Main Street Station, Daytona Beach
No Name Lounge, Panama City
No Name Pub, Big Pine Key
Papa Joe's, Islamorada
Safari Lounge, Caloosa Cove, the Keys
Snapper's, Key Largo
Tobacco Road, Miami

Restaurants

Boss Oyster, Apalachicola
Casa Tina's, Dunedin
The Fish House, Key Largo
Islamorada Restaurant & Bakery, Islamorada
Joanie's Blue Crab Cafe, Ochopee

Mangrove Mama's, Sugarloaf Key
Pollo Tropical, various locations
Seven Mile Grille, Marathon
Shivers, Homestead
Sonny's Real Pit Bar-B-Que, various locations

Herb Hastings of Herb's Limestone Grocery
and Country Club, Limestone

Further Reading

Books

Andrews, J. J. C. *The Well-Built Elephant and Other Roadside Attractions: A Tribute to American Eccentricity.* New York: Congdon and Weed, 1984.

Baeder, John. *Sign Language: Street Signs as Folk Art.* New York: Abrams, 1996.

Breslauer, Ken. *Roadside Paradise: The Golden Age of Florida's Tourist Attractions, 1929–71.* St. Petersburg: RetroFlorida, 2000.

Brouws, Jeff, Bernd Polster, and Phil Patton. *Highway: America's Endless Dream.* New York: Stewart, Tabori and Chang, 1997.

Butko, Brian, and Sarah Butko. *Roadside Giants.* Mechanicsburg, PA: Stackpole Books, 2005.

Congdon, Kristin G., and Tina Bucuvalas. *Just above the Water: Florida Folk Art.* Jackson: University of Mississippi Press, 2006.

Davidson, Len. *Vintage Neon.* Atglen, PA: Schiffer, 1999.

Evans, Walker. *Signs*. Los Angeles: J. Paul Getty Museum, 1998.

Gallant, Frank K. *A Place Called Peculiar: Stories about Unusual Place Names*. Springfield, MA: Merriam-Webster, 1998.

Genovese, Peter. *The Great American Road Trip: US 1, Maine to Florida*. New Brunswick, NJ: Rutgers University Press, 1999.

———. *Roadside New Jersey*. New Brunswick, NJ: Rutgers University Press, 1994.

Gladstone, Gary. *Passing Gas. And Other Towns along the American Highway*. Berkeley, CA: Ten Speed Press, 2003.

Glasgow, Vaughn L. *A Social History of the American Alligator*. New York: St. Martin's Press, 1991.

Graham, Alistair, and Peter Beard. *Eyelids of Morning: The Mingled Destinies of Crocodiles and Men*. 1974. Reprint, San Francisco: Chronicle Books, 1990.

Grimes, David, and Tom Becnel. *Florida Curiosities*. Guilford, CT: Globe Pequot Press, 2003.

Heimann, Jim. *California Crazy and Beyond: Roadside Vernacular Architecture*. San Francisco: Chronicle Books, 2001.

Hobson, Archie, ed. *Remembering America: A Sampler of the WPA American Guide Series*. New York: Columbia University Press, 1985.

Hollis, Tim. *Dixie before Disney: 100 Years of Roadside Fun*. Jackson: University Press of Mississippi, 1999.

———. *Florida's Miracle Strip: From Redneck Riviera to Emerald Coast*. Jackson: University Press of Mississippi, 2004.

———. *Glass Bottom Boats and Mermaid Tails: Florida's Tourist Springs*. Mechanicsburg, PA: Stackpole Books, 2006.

Jensen, Jamie. *Road Trip USA: Cross-Country Adventures on America's Two-Lane Highways*. Emeryville, CA: Avalon Travel, 2002.

Kitchen, Dennis. *Our Smallest Towns: Big Falls, Blue Eye, Bonanza and Beyond*. San Francisco: Chronicle Books, 1995.

Kuralt, Charles. *Dateline America*. New York: Harcourt Brace Jovanovich, 1979.

Margolies, John. *Fun along the Road: American Tourist Attractions*. Boston: Bullfinch Press, 1998.

———. *Home Away from Home: Motels in America*. Boston: Bullfinch Press, 1995.

Margolies, John, Nina Garfinkel, and Maria Reidelbach. *Miniature Golf*. New York: Abbeville Press, 1987.

Marling, Karal Ann. *The Colossus of Roads: Myth and Symbol Along the American Highway*. Minneapolis: University of Minnesota Press, 1984.

McGovern, Bernie, ed. *Florida Almanac*. Gretna, LA: Pelican Publishing, 2004.

Pohlen, Jerome. *Oddball Florida*. Chicago: Chicago Review Press, 2004.

Rowsome, Frank, Jr. *The Verse by the Side of the Road*. New York: Plume, 1965.

Thomasson, Sylvia McCardel. *I Am Ruby*. Atlanta: Cardel Press, 2004.

Magazine

American Road. Mock Turtle Press, Mount Clemons, MI, www.mockturtlepress.com.

Websites

Roadside America: www.roadsideamerica.com.

Ghost Towns: www.ghosttowns.com.

Acknowledgments

For this book, I used the same technique—or rather, lack of one—I used in earlier books. I've always found that dropping in on people works better than scheduled visits and interviews. You can be anyone on the phone. In person, you can make your case, show someone you're real and genuine. Never once did any of the folks I interviewed for this book tell me to go away or come back another time. I drove thousands and thousands of miles around Florida, and spent more nights on the road than I care to remember, but the friendliness, hospitality, and kindness I was shown from Pensacola to Key West made this a fun project.

Special thanks to the following people:

Eli Sfassie, Kathy Franco, and Karen Potocnak at Orange World in Kissimmee, the World's Largest Orange, for all their help and juicy information. And yes, next time I'll bring a ladder.

James Irvine and the rest of the Men from Mars, for coming back down to earth and answering my questions.

Howard Solomon, the king of Solomon's Castle, for the behind-the-scenes tour of his amazing complex.

Nanette Watson, postmaster at Ochopee Post Office, the nation's smallest, for taking time out to answer my questions, and Alex de Quesada and his daughter Nikki for their help.

The extraordinary Ruby Williams, farmer and artist, still going strong after all these years. I hope I have half her energy in five—much less thirty—years.

Patty and Allen Register at Gatorama in Palmdale, for the tour of their classic roadside attraction.

Larry Deitch, minister of the Drive-in Christian Church in Daytona Beach Shores, for taking the time out—on Christmas Day, no less—to tell the story of his one-of-a-kind church.

Dave Shealy, the man behind the Skunk Ape Research Headquarters, for recounting all those hair-raising stories about the Everglades "Sasquatch."

The guys at Mad Hatter Muffler in Miami and Hollywood: Steve Pearl, for his help, and Kevin Doyle, the muffler artist, for showing me his work—and letting me buy one of his frogs!

The late Donald Ferguson, who owned Fergie's Fruit and Color World in Leesburg, the most beautiful roadside market in Florida.

Nina Johnson at the Bernice Steinbaum Gallery in Miami, for steering me to Michael Tronn of the Urban Art Farm.

Jimbo Luznar, owner of Jimbo's in Virginia Key, and the friendliest man in Florida, for telling his life story, pretty much nonstop, one Saturday morning. I'm going to try to get to your birthday party next April!

Marsha at Raccoon River Camp Resort in Panama City Beach, for the vintage postcards of Goofy Golf.

Bryan Fitzell at Maroone Dodge in Miami, for quickly getting my usually reliable Jeep back on the road.

And Kyle Weaver, editor at Stackpole Books. Several years ago, Kyle approached me about writing a book for Stackpole; we met at Mastoris Diner in New Jersey. He had his heart set on a guide to diners. I told him the book I really wanted to write was roadside Florida, a subject that had not been given its due. Kyle, fortunately, said yes, and I want to thank him for the beautiful book you now have in your hands.

Index

About the Author

Peter Genovese is a feature writer for *The Star-Ledger* of Newark, New Jersey, for which he oversees the popular Munchmobile series (www.nj.com/munchmobile), and a regular contributor to *American Road* magazine. He is the author of *Roadside New Jersey*; *Jersey Diners*; *The Great American Road Trip: US 1, Maine to Florida*; *New Jersey Curiosities*; *The Jersey Shore Uncovered: A Revealing Season on the Beach*; and *The Food Lover's Guide to New Jersey*. *New Jersey Monthly* magazine named him "One of 40 New Jerseyans We Love."